TO KNOW HIS NAME

Knowing God Through His Names

*"And those who know Your name will put their trust in You,
For You, O Lord, have not forsaken those who seek You."*

Psalm 9:10

Name _____

To Know His Name

Knowing God Through His Names

About To Know His Name

Beginning with creation, God has revealed His character by using descriptive names— names such as El Shaddai – the Everlasting God; Jehovah Jireh – the Lord will Provide; Adonai – Lord, Master; and Jehovah-Nissi – the Lord is my Banner. Through His names, God also reveals His provision, power, and His heart of love for His people. As we begin to understand the names of God, we will know Him more intimately and we will be encouraged to trust God and to turn to Him in times of trial (Psalm 9:10). We will worship and praise Him genuinely (Psalm 48:10), love Him more deeply, and share who He is with others. *To Know His Name* covers 19 unique names for God in a 22-week study. Each week is broken down into five separate days. Each study will look at the first time that name is revealed in Scripture and the impact knowing God by that name has for women's lives today.

FIVE DAY FORMAT

Each lesson is broken down into five separate days. This is only a recommended way to divide your study. A woman may use this breakdown or another of her choosing.

MEMORY VERSE

Each lesson will include a memory verse on page 2. The memory verse should be learned for the week the lesson is discussed in your group.

DEEPER KNOWLEDGE

Most lessons will have a section labeled "Deeper Knowledge." These optional sections provide the opportunity for additional study.

To Know His Name
Copyright © 2014 by Salem Heights Church Women's Ministries
All rights reserved.

Scripture taken from the NEW AMERICAN STANDARD BIBLE®, Copyright © 1960,1962,1963,1968,1971,1972,1973,1975,1977,1995 by The Lockman Foundation. Used by permission.

All artwork is used by permission. All rights reserved.

Written by the Salem Heights Church Curriculum Writing Team and Editing Team: Karen Bain, Lauren Bain, Julie Bernard, Tara Cox, Linda Davis, Emily Dempster, Jenn Elliot, Angi Greene, Becky Griffiths, Cindy Helsley, Jennean Hill, Donna Hodge, DeAnna Jones, Julie McGinty, Karin Penn, Lynn Piper, Erin Rowzee, Celeste Starr, Gina Weigand, Pam Williams.

Contributing Authors
To Know His Name

Emily Dempster *is serving as the Curriculum Coordinator for Salem Heights Church Women's Ministries. She earned her Master's Degree in Pastoral Counseling through Liberty Theological Seminary University. She has a passion for discipleship in the church and seeing women's lives changed as a result of God's Word. When given the chance, Emily loves skiing, hiking and fishing in Central Oregon with her husband and two children.*

Julie Bernard *serves as the Women's Ministry Director at Salem Heights Church. She loves the team approach to ministry and encouraging and developing Women's Ministry leaders. She enjoys drinking coffee with friends, snuggling with her four grandchildren, and golfing with her husband.*

Tara Cox *currently serves as the Girls' Night Out Coordinator for Salem Heights Church Women's Ministry. She graduated from Corban University with a B.S. in Biblical Studies and is hoping to complete her Master's Degree. She spends most of her time chasing, dancing, reading to and otherwise growing up her three girls alongside her husband. She has a passion to see others come to know and love God through the study of His Word.*

Linda Davis *has been actively involved in Bible Study Fellowship for many years, serving as both discussion leader and teacher. Her summers are filled with ministry work as a local host for the National Bible Bee, an organization aimed at equipping parents to disciple their families. Linda, wife and homeschooling mom of three, increasingly finds her greatest passion and fulfillment in pointing others to the sufficiency of the Scriptures.*

Angi Greene *serves with college-age students in the Cross Road Ministry at Salem Heights Church. She is also involved in Biblical Counseling and enjoys ministering with her husband to couples preparing for marriage. She treasures opportunities to disciple and mentor women as she encourages them to love God and His Word. She loves spending time with her husband, daughter and two sons. Reading, running and baking are a few of her hobbies.*

Rebecca Griffiths *loves to study God's Word and witness how the lives of women are impacted as they interact with God and His truth. She is a wife and mom of two boys, and serves as a leader in the Salem Heights Church Discipleship program. Rebecca and her family love nature and enjoy the beautiful state of Oregon by way of hiking, canoeing, camping, or backpacking.*

Jennean Hill *is Art's wife of 37 years, mother of two, grandmother of five and full-time homemaker. She has had a love for the Word of God since early childhood and has a deep desire to exhort others in the love and knowledge of our Savior. This has been a natural lead into Bible study and discipleship of other women. Her 23 years at Salem Heights Church have allowed her leadership roles and ministry opportunities through music, tech, drama, and writing. Besides family and friends, three of her favorite interests are flowers, antiques, and visiting places she's never been before.*

Julie McGinty *is a retired R.N. who has taught piano in her home for over forty years. She loves delving into intensive personal Bible study, as well as encouraging other women to do the same by serving as a facilitator for Women's Discipleship Studies. Julie loves serving on her church Music Team, spending time with her grandchildren, and aerobic walking.*

Karin Penn *considers herself a Californegonian since settling in Oregon after college. She has been deeply impacted by the teaching at Salem Heights Church and loves attending there with her husband and two boys. She loves to crack a good joke and make people laugh. She feels privileged to have been able to serve in Women's Ministries for almost twenty years.*

Lynn Piper *enjoys serving in the CAUSE high school ministry at Salem Heights Church. Discipling and watching God grow the youth brings her great joy. She has a Master's Degree in Teaching Mathematics. Gardening, running, hiking and playing with her boys are her favorite free time activities.*

Pam Williams *has a degree in Psychology from Corban University and is currently involved in Biblical Counseling/Mentoring at Salem Heights Church as well as www.settingcaptivesfree.com. Her passion is to not only see marriages healed and restored, but to encourage women to be diligently practicing what they know to be true from God's Word. Pam is married and has three daughters and one son-in-law. She loves camping, biking and hiking with them. After taking eighteen years off to raise her daughters, she is back to work as an instructional assistant with special needs children.*

Other Contributors - *Karen Bain, Lauren Bain, Jenn Elliott, Cindy Helsley, Donna Hodge, DeAnna Jones, Erin Rowzee, Celeste Starr, Gina Weigand.*

Table of Contents
To Know His Name

Lesson 1	Introduction to the Names		
Lesson 2	Elohim	Mighty Creator	El-lo-HEEM
Lesson 3	Yahweh	LORD, Jehovah	Yah-WEH
Lesson 4	El	God of Power and Might	EL
Lesson 5	El Elyon	God Most High	El-El-YOHN
Lesson 6	Adonai	Lord and Master	Ad-do-NI
Lesson 7	El Roi	God Who Sees	El-raw-EE
Lesson 8	El Shaddai	God Almighty	El-shad-DAI
Lesson 9	El Olam	God Everlasting	El-o-LAM
Lesson 10	Jehovah Jireh	The Lord Will Provide	Jehovah Ji-RAH
Lesson 11	El Bethel	God Our Home	El Beth-EL
Lesson 12	Jehovah Rophe	The Lord Heals	Jehovah Row-FEH
Lesson 13	Jehovah Nissi	The Lord My Banner	Jehovah Nis-SEE
Lesson 14	Jehovah M'Kadesh	The Lord Who Sanctifies	Jehovah Mah-KA-desh
Lesson 15	Jehovah Shalom	The Lord Is Peace	Jehovah Sha-LOME
Lesson 16	Jehovah Sabaoth	The Lord of Hosts	Jehovah Sa-ba-OTH
Lesson 17	Jehovah Raah	The Lord My Shepherd	Jehovah Ra-AH
Lesson 18	Jehovah Tsidkenu	The Lord Our Righteousness	Jehovah Sid-KA-nu
Lesson 19	Jehovah Shammah	The Lord is There	Jehovah SHAM-mah
Lesson 20	Pater	Father	Pat-AYR
Lesson 21	Conclusion - Part 1		
Lesson 22	Conclusion - Part 2		

Knowing God Through His Names

TO KNOW HIS NAME
An Introduction

Do you Twitter? Have a MySpace page? Collect friends on Facebook? Social networking websites are all the rage. At the core of this Internet phenomenon is our need for relationships. While you can follow hundreds of "Tweeple" in the "Twitterverse," chat in the latest MySpace lingo, or reconnect with your college roommate on Facebook, only the Lord will completely satisfy. Like the thousand-piece puzzle ruined by one oddly shaped hole in the middle, our lives are not the masterpiece God intended without an intimate, vibrant relationship with Him. That one piece makes all the difference!

Such knowledge of our Maker is the essence of eternal life: *"This is eternal life, that they may know You, the only true God, and Jesus Christ whom You have sent"* (John 17:3). It's not enough that God knows us; He wants us to know Him. Possessing this knowledge of Him yields life with meaning, life with eternal significance. We need to stop thinking of eternal life as something future. To know God is to live—really live—NOW!

In Genesis 2:18, God set forth the principle: *"It is not good for the man to be alone...."* Convinced of this truth, we have sought meaningful relationships, but how many people do we really know? The Internet makes it easier to know *about* friends, but do we really *know* them? Similarly, we can go to church, hang out with Christians, even attend a Bible study, but do these activities guarantee true knowledge of God?

So, how do we come to know true friendship with God? Scripture promises that if we seek Him, we will find Him. God wants to be found. Since Genesis 1:1, God has been revealing Himself to man through His various names, each revealing who He is, why we should trust Him, and why we so desperately need Him.

What are you seeking that no other relationship has satisfied? Are you looking for healing, safety, peace, guidance, or cleansing? Do you desire a friend who is always there and never lets you down? Whatever your need, the provision is God. To know His name is to know true friendship with Him. *"And those who know Your name will put their trust in You, for You, O LORD, have not forsaken those who seek You"* (Psalm 9:10).

Day 1
What's in a Name?

If you are a mother, most likely you put some thought into what name you gave your child. Perhaps you considered passing on a family name, or maybe you based your decision on the special way it sounded when coupled with your last name. Names given in Bible times identified the person and reflected his nature and character. For example, Naomi (pleasant) changed her name to Mara (bitter) after suffering great loss. Isaac (laughter) was named for his mother's response to the unbelievable news of his birth. Barnabas' name (son of encouragement) reflected his gift to others.

1. Find the meaning of your name. How does it suit you, or how does it not?

2. Each woman comes to this study with her own view of God. Who is God? How would you describe Him? How have you come to this conclusion?

We can learn about Who God is, His character and nature, by studying His names in Scripture, names such as El Shaddai (God Almighty); Jehovah Jireh (the Lord Will Provide); and El Roi (the God Who Sees). From the very first verse, God has made Himself known by specific names, each revealed at a specific time, in a specific circumstance, and for a specific purpose. To know His name is to know God!

GOD'S NAME IS IMPORTANT

> Read Exodus 20:7

3. In this list of important commandments, explain what God says about His Name?

   Why do you think He would specifically include this commandment?

Memory Verse

"And those who know Your name will put their trust in You, for You, O LORD, have not forsaken those who seek You."

Psalm 9:10

4. What are specific ways a person can honor the Name of the Lord?

How are you honoring His name? What more should you be doing?

Read Leviticus 24:10-23

5. Describe the offense and consequence depicted in this passage.

6. What does God want us to learn about His name from this incident?

7. How does today's lesson inspire you to know and reverence God's name?

Day 2

To Know His Name Is to Know Him

GOD WANTS TO BE KNOWN

Knowing God's name is synonymous with knowing God Himself. Recorded in Scripture are various people to whom God revealed Himself, establishing with each a uniquely personal relationship. Why do we remember these great people of God? Because they knew Him! Their relationship with God defined them.

Key Term

The three primary names of God are: El, Adonai, and Jehovah (literally YHWH or Yahweh). Many of God's names combine either El or Jehovah to form secondary names. Each of these compound names retain the full meaning of the primary, while adding the emphasis of the second word.

8. Who is one person in Scripture who knew God? What was unique about God's relationship with His friend?

GOD REVEALS HIMSELF IN HIS WORD

While God employed special revelation to initiate and develop His relationship with each "friend," such was not His ultimate plan for making Himself known. Today, God primarily reveals Himself to us through His Word.

Read 2 Kings 23:1-28

Prior to this passage, the long-forgotten Book of the Law was discovered and presented to King Josiah.

9. Without the Book of the Law, Judah had strayed far from God. What sort of sins had Judah committed in verses 4-24?

What sins do you observe today by those who ignore God's Word?

10. Explain how the discovery of the Book of the Law changed the relationship between God and Judah.

How has knowing and obeying God's Word shaped your relationship with Him?

11. Reading God's Word inspired Josiah to take drastic action against sin. Record his acts of obedience.

How has knowledge of God's Word inspired you to live differently than those who ignore His written revelation?

12. How is Josiah remembered (verse 25)?

13. God desires you to know Him through His Word. What steps are you taking to fulfill His desire?

14. What specific commitment will you make this year to know His name? What is your motivation? What are your expectations?

Day 3

To Know His Name Is to Know Jesus

If knowledge of God's name is knowing God...
And if God's Word is the source for learning His name...
And if "the Word became flesh" as John 1:14 teaches regarding Jesus...

THEN...To know God's name is to know Jesus.

"[T]he name of Jesus Christ is invested with every attribute that 'the name of the Lord' implied in the Old Testament, it was in that name that the apostles went everywhere preaching, and it was that name which unbelievers feared."[1]

15. How is Jesus' deity described in each of the following passages?

   John 1:1-3

   John 1:18

   Philippians 2:5-8

   Colossians 1:15

   Colossians 2:9

   Hebrews 1:1-3

   Summarize the core truth of these passages.

A Psalm of David

"The law of the LORD is perfect, restoring the soul; the testimony of the LORD is sure, making wise the simple. The precepts of the LORD are right, rejoicing the heart; the commandment of the LORD is pure, enlightening the eyes. The fear of the LORD is clean, enduring forever; the judgments of the LORD are true; they are righteous altogether. They are more desirable than gold, yes, than much fine gold; sweeter also than honey and the drippings of the honeycomb. Moreover, by them Your servant is warned; in keeping them there is great reward. "

Psalm 19:7-11

Read John 14:1-8

16. In what ways does Jesus present Himself as equal to the Father?

17. What does Jesus say in verse 4, and what is Thomas' response?

    What does Jesus say in verse 7, and what is Philip's response?

18. What do you learn about Thomas and Philip from their responses to Jesus? Why do you think they questioned Jesus' clear revelation of Himself? How should they have responded?

    In what ways have you been like Thomas and Philip?

Read John 14:9-11

19. What do you learn about Jesus' relationship to the Father?

20. From what you learned today, explain "To Know God's Name Is to Know Jesus."

If knowledge of God's name is knowing God…

And if God's Word is the source for learning His name…

And if "the Word became flesh" as John 1:14 teaches regarding Jesus…

THEN…To know God's name is to know Jesus.

21. In verse 9, Jesus said: "He who has seen Me has seen the Father." What has the Father revealed about Himself to you through Jesus in the past? This week? Today?

22. How has knowing God personally through faith in Jesus given your life an eternal quality?

   What can you do to know Jesus more intimately?

Day 4

To Know His Name Is to Trust Him

Read Psalm 20

23. What is contrasted in verse 7?

   What might be the contemporary equivalent to trusting in chariots and horses?

24. In what ways have you trusted in chariots and horses? In what ways are you now trusting in the name of the Lord?

"He who has seen Me has seen the Father."
John 14:9

Read Psalm 9:10 (Key verse for the study)

25. What does this verse tell us about God?

26. In what area of your life do you need to develop trust in the Lord?

27. What is your specific plan to more diligently and deliberately seek the Lord this year?

Read Proverbs 18:10

28. What qualities does a strong tower have?

29. What promise applies to the righteous in this proverb?

30. Look at the list of names and meanings in the sidebar on the next page. To what names might you run for protection?

   To what names might you run when you need strength?

   To what names might you run when you are fearful?

   To what names might you run when you need encouragement?

   What name are you most excited to study this year? Why?

> "Some trust in chariots and some in horses, but we trust in the name of the LORD our God."
> Psalm 20:7, NIV

Day 5
To Know His Name Is to Worship Him

WORSHIP BEGINS WITH LOVE

31. What command does God give to believers in Matthew 22:37? (The Greek word for love in this verse is *agapao,* which means to love out of devotion and commitment.)

   How will studying the names of God help you to fulfill this command?

32. Read Psalm 5:11 and Psalm 91:14. What relationship exists between knowing God's name and loving Him?

33. Write a prayer of commitment to God, asking Him to help you not only learn intellectually His names, but to also grow your love for who He is this year.

LET THE PRAISING BEGIN

We can better know how to worship God when we understand His name. He is worthy of our praise.

The Names of God

Elohim - God, Mighty Creator

El - God of Power and Might

El Elyon - God Most High

Adonai - Lord and Master

El Roi - God Who Sees

El Shaddai - God Almighty

El Olam - God Everlasting

El Bethel - God Our Home

Yahweh - LORD, Jehovah

Jehovah Jireh - The Lord Will Provide

Jehovah Rophe - The Lord Heals

Jehovah Nissi - The Lord My Banner

Jehovah M'Kadesh - The Lord Who Sanctifies

Jehovah Shalom - The Lord Is Peace

Jehovah-Sabaoth - The Lord of Hosts

Jehovah-Raah - The Lord My Shepherd

Jehovah-Tsidkenu - The Lord Our Righteousness

Jehovah-Shammah - The Lord Is There

Abba Pater - Father

34. The Psalms include many passages on worshiping God's name. For each psalm, summarize the way God's name is praised.

   Psalm 18:49

   Psalm 29:2

   Psalm 48:10

   Psalm 52:9

   Psalm 63:4

   Find a few more on your own. List them here.

35. What worship song comes to mind when you consider praising the Lord. Note here any lyrics you remember.

36. Write your own praise worshiping the name of the Lord.

Experiencing Knowledge

37. What are you most looking forward to in this study?

   What impact do you hope this study will have on your relationship with God?

Reflection

Knowing God Through His Names Lesson Two

ELOHIM
Mighty Creator

Have you ever looked at the night sky and wondered in awe at the vastness of the universe? Our galaxy alone boasts an estimated one hundred billion stars. Multiplied by the several hundred thousand million known galaxies, the number of stars roughly totals 10,000,000,000,000,000,000,000,000 or 10^{25}. Such massive figures surpass our comprehension. Certainly only God knows the exact number of stars (Psalm 147:4; Jeremiah 33:22). Contemplating just this one detail of creation, we begin to appreciate its immensity, its complexity. Only God could have done this!

Just as we marvel at the universe, with similar effort we grapple with and try to answer the big questions of life. "How did everything around us come into being?" "Why are we here?" Apart from God, man in his quest for answers offers only opinion at the expense of truth. But how can such principles of creation be understood apart from the only One whose opinion matters—the One who formed it all? Studying Elohim through Scripture's account of creation answers those tough who, how, what, and why questions.

Fittingly, God first introduces Himself to man in Genesis 1:1 as Elohim, the beginning of all things. Scripture further emphasizes what we learn from creation, God's supremacy over and distinction from man. We, like the psalmist, might ask, *"When I consider Your heavens, the work of Your fingers, the moon and the stars, which You have ordained; what is man that You take thought of him, and the son of man that You care for him?"* (Psalm 8:3-4). The very fact that God created us reveals our significance, our worth to Him. Furthermore, what profound truth that the Maker of the countless stars, the One who holds the answer to every difficult question, Mighty Creator Elohim, wants to be known by us!

Day 1
God Creates the Universe

THE "WHO"

1. Have you ever received a personalized, handmade gift just for you? What made it special?

In Genesis 1:1, the beginning of the epic story of all time, we are introduced to the protagonist Elohim—"God" in our Bibles. Yet to call Him a mere character in a story is to miss the fullness of Who He is. He is the Author, the all-powerful Creator, the Designer, Master, Savior, the God of gods, the Beginning and the End, and indeed much more!

> **Read Genesis 1:1-25**

You may want to substitute "Elohim" or "Mighty Creator" for God as you read. Try reading the passage as if it were the first time.

2. From Genesis 1:1-25 record text-specific observations about God's actions and His creation. Pay particular attention to repeated phrases, contrasts and conclusions.

GOD	CREATION

Memory Verse

"'Worthy are You, our Lord and our God, to receive glory and honor and power; for You created all things, and because of Your will they existed, and were created.'"

Revelation 4:11

Key Term

Elohim: General term for god, gods, ruler, judge. Used over 2,300 times in the Old Testament, this plural form of El means powerful, mighty, strong one. Because Elohim is introduced and used extensively in the Creation account (some 28 times in the first chapter alone), many scholars have come to identify and define Elohim as Powerful God, Creator.

3. What does this biblical account of creation reveal about Elohim? What new (or renewed) thought do you have about His character?

4. Record phrases or words of praise to the Creator in the following verses:

    Psalm 8:3-9

    Psalm 33:8-9

    Psalm 95:4-6

    Jeremiah 32:17

    Write your own words of praise to the Creator.

5. Envision yourself standing on a mountain top, at the ocean's vast edge, beneath a dramatic sunset, or under a canopy of glittering stars. And consider the unmistakable evidence of Divine handiwork in the beauty of a flower, the power of a storm, the miracle of new life. What do you learn about Elohim the Mighty Creator from your own observations of creation today?

Notes

6. How do these observations from Scripture and personal experience lead you to greater worship of Elohim?

> ### Deeper Knowledge
>
> Use a concordance or topical Bible to research the use of the word "light" in Scripture.
>
> Why do you think Elohim's first creative act on earth was "light" (v. 3)?

Day 2

"In the beginning Elohim bara . . ."

THE "HOW"
GOD CREATED...OUT OF NOTHING

Read Genesis 1:1-25

7. Using a dictionary, define the word "create," and compare and contrast it with the term "bara." What conclusions do you draw regarding how creation happened?

Key Term

Bara: To fashion, shape, or create; to bring into existence; to create out of nothing. Used in this tense, the term is reserved solely to describe God's initiation of something altogether new.

...BY HIS WORD

8. While bearing in mind the repeated phrase "And God said" in the Genesis passage, read Psalm 33:6-7, 9; and 148:5-6. Tell how God accomplished the creation of the material universe, and what this observation reveals about Elohim.

9. God could have thought the world into existence, but He chose to create it through His spoken Word. Today God speaks through Scripture, His written Word. Read John 1:1-3, 14 and Hebrews 11:3. What truths about God's Word are revealed in these verses, and how do they underscore the importance of Scripture?

10. What place does God's Word have in your life? What specific actions reveal the importance you place on it?

...WITH POWER AND AUTHORITY

11. Next to each reference, indicate where God's power and authority are displayed.

    Job 34:19

    Psalm 65:6

    Psalm 90:2

    Psalm 94:9

    Psalm 121:2

    Psalm 136:5-9

    Psalm 146:5-6

    Proverbs 3:19

    Isaiah 44:24

Notes

How do these demonstrations of His power and authority impact the way you view your current circumstances and trials?

...AND IT WAS GOOD!

12. God declared His creation "good." Explain what you think God means by "good."

> God is Mighty Creator and all that He created was good.

13. Take a moment to reflect on the profound truth that God is Mighty Creator and all that He created was good. Write a short prayer of thanksgiving and worship.

Day 3

God Created Mankind
THE "WHAT"

Isaiah 45:18 says, "...[the LORD] did not create [the earth] empty, He formed it to be inhabited!" (ESV) Evident in God's plan and purpose for creation is His desire for an intimate relationship with man.

> Read Genesis 1:26-2:9

14. Record your observations about the creation of man from these verses.

15. How would you say this passage reflects God's surpassing affection for mankind in comparison to how He regards the rest of creation?

16. Using the sidebar explanation of "image," describe how man is made in God's image. Include specific ways man is similar to and different from God.

17. Of all creation, only mankind is made in God's image. Reflect on the significance of this truth.

18. Note that both male and female are made in God's image. What does this fact mean to you as a woman, and how does this knowledge impact your relationship with God?

19. Read John 3:16 and 1 Timothy 2:1-4. Think of someone you know who is lost without God. Knowing he or she was created in God's image, how will you change your attitude and the way you interact with this person?

Key Term

Image: Likeness, resemblance, idol. "*Selem* [image] does not signify an exact duplicate, but only the shadow of the thing, representing the original in an imprecise manner and lacking the essential characteristics of the original."[1]

Day 4
God Created YOU

THE "WHY"

God created YOU—personally, purposely, uniquely, and intricately. You are an original design, never to be duplicated! Reflect on this truth as we examine God's very personal creation of each human being in Psalm 139:13-16 (below). As you read, note the meaning of certain key words provided in parentheses.

"For You **formed** (*to form, create, as a master potter*) my inward parts; You **wove** (*to weave, interweave, weave together*) me in my mother's womb.

I will give thanks to You, for I am **fearfully** (*in a wonderful manner; to cause astonishment and awe*) and **wonderfully** (*to become distinguished, admirable, separate from, marked out*) made; **Wonderful** (*beyond one's power, difficult to do or understand, extraordinary*) are Your works, and my soul knows it very well.

My **frame** (*bones*) was not hidden from You, when I was made in **secret** (*covering, shelter, hiding place, place of protection*), and **skillfully wrought** (*to adorn with colors, variegate, as with needlework or embroidery*) in the depths of the earth;

Your eyes have **seen** (*to see, look at, perceive, inspect, consider; regard, look after, learn about, observe, watch, look upon; give attention to, gaze at; behold*) my unformed substance; and in Your book were all written the days that were **ordained** (*to form in the mind, plan, devise; to be predestined*) for me, when as yet there was not one of them."[2]

20. What does this passage reveal about God and His creation of each human being?

21. Which key words most impact your heart? (Pick at least three to explain.)

Notes

22. How do the following verses further illustrate the personal nature of God's creation of you?

    Psalm 100:3

    Jeremiah 1:5

    Ephesians 1:4-5, 2:10

23. Describe God's opinion of you personally. How would you say you are resting in "His opinion"? How does your life reflect contentment with how God made you?

24. What do you most want to change about yourself or your circumstances? How might God be desiring to fulfill His purpose through this area of discontentment? What commitment will you make to adopt God's perspective in this area?

25. According to this week's memory verse, God created you uniquely to accomplish His will; His specific design of you is essential to His plan. In what areas do you see God using you to fulfill His purpose?

26. From today's study, what has Elohim revealed to you personally about His creation of you?

Notes

27. Recognizing and receiving the truth that we are special to God should motivate us to know Him more. What specifically can you do to grow even closer to Him?

Day 5

Our Response to Elohim as New Creations

Through studying the name Elohim in Scripture, we've received God's answers to many of life's big questions, namely the Who, how, what, and why of creation. Now let's turn our attention to application, specifically how God reveals Himself as Elohim to us today through the creative work of Jesus Christ.

28. What do you learn about Jesus' role in creation from the following verses: 1 Corinthians 8:6; Colossians 1:16-17; Hebrews 1:2?

29. Compare Genesis 2:7 and Ephesians 2:1-5. How is Jesus the full revelation of Elohim? Include in your answer a discussion of the parallels between Elohim's original creation of mankind and Jesus' new creation of fallen humanity.

30. What do these verses indicate is Jesus' purpose in giving you spiritual life?

    Romans 6:4

    2 Corinthians 5:17

    Ephesians 2:10

    Ephesians 4:17-24

    Colossians 3:10

Notes

31. Examine your own life, and record the evidence of Jesus' new creation in you.

32. How will you specifically express your gratitude to Jesus for making you new?

Experiencing Knowledge

33. Including principles from Revelation 4:11 and Isaiah 43:7, create a purpose statement for your life as a new creation.

34. What one change could you make to more closely follow your life's purpose statement?

35. How does knowledge of this name of God lead you to put your trust in Him (Psalm 9:10)? What specifically will you do today to demonstrate this trust in Elohim?

Reflection

Knowing God Through His Names 

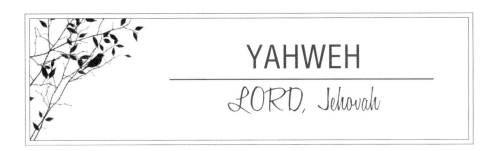

YAHWEH
LORD, Jehovah

It's going to be a great birthday! You've scheduled coffee and crepes with your girlfriend, followed by shopping and pedicures. Dinner promises to be equally fabulous, as Hubby is taking you to that new restaurant in town. And you're especially intrigued by the obvious excitement about the gift he's bought you. Yes, it's going to be a wonderful day!

You jump out of bed, heading down to the laundry room to get your favorite blouse. About six feet from the door, your toes no longer feel dry, fluffy carpeting. Oh, no! Oh, yes! Apparently, that late-night load of laundry did not go well. The laundry room and half the hallway are soaked! So much for breakfast with your friend! You'll be stuck at home today waiting for the repairman. Well, at least there's still dinner and that present!

By late afternoon, life is back on track. Let's bring on Date night! Showered and dressed in your favorite blouse, you wait ... and wait. Where is he? He should have been home by now. Finally, the phone rings! Hubby has been called into a last-minute emergency meeting. He promises to make it up to you ... tomorrow.

It's quite late when he gets home, but he does arrive carrying THE gift! It's certainly too large to be jewelry. What could it possibly be? You tear into the paper and immediately comprehend why your husband has been so giddy. It's a new cordless drill! This day turned out nothing like you expected. What a disappointment!

It has been said: "Blessed is he that expects nothing, for he shall never be disappointed." [1739 B. Franklin Poor Richard's Almanack (May)] Days like these certainly support this maxim. Perhaps this was how Moses felt after shepherding his father-in-law's flock for forty years in the land of Midian. He had once lived as royalty in the palace of Pharaoh. He thought he had been set apart for great things! Life was not at all as Moses expected. What a disappointment!

Or so it seemed ... until God unveiled Himself to Moses as "Yahweh." Tough circumstances can cause disappointment, God reveals that our expectations of Him can never exceed who He is, for God is always so much more!

Day 1
The LORD Is Personal

1. Recall a time when your unmet expectations led to disappointment. What lesson(s) did you learn from this experience?

BACKGROUND ON YAHWEH (LORD Jehovah)

Most Bible scholars agree that Yahweh, occurring 6,823 times in Scripture, is the proper name of God. Considered too holy to be spoken, ancient scribes excluded vowels, writing only YHWH to represent this name of God. In oral reading of Scripture, Jews inserted the vowels from Adonai (Hebrew for "Lord") to make YaHoWaH (our "Jehovah.") To distinguish "Yahweh" from "Adonai," English translators write "LORD" for the former, and "Lord" for the latter.

The word "Yahweh" comes from the Hebrew verb "to be," introduced as "I AM" in Exodus 3:14. Included in the concept of God as "I AM" is His self-existence (the uncaused cause). Among God's other attributes revealed in the name "I AM," are His eternality and self-sufficiency. In addition, "I AM" captures God's essence as real, unchangeable, and self-fulfilled. Finally, perhaps the most significant meaning of Yahweh is God's desire to reveal Himself to man. Whether used alone, or combined with His other descriptive names, Yahweh is above all the personal God of revelation.[1]

> Read Genesis 2:4-9, 15-25

Note: Yahweh is translated in capital letters as "LORD." You may find it helpful to mark "LORD" and "God" (Elohim) with distinct marks in today's reading.

2. What creative acts are described in these verses?

Which one is emphasized?

Memory Verse

"God said to Moses, 'I AM WHO I AM;' and He said, 'Thus you shall say to the sons of Israel, 'I AM has sent me to you.'"

Exodus 3:14

Jews inserted the vowels from Adonai (Hebrew for "Lord") to make YaHoWaH (our "Jehovah"). The names that are paired with Jehovah, (i.e. Jehovah Jireh) use Yahweh as the root of the name.

3. Genesis 2:4 records the first occurrence of "Yahweh" in Scripture. From Genesis 1 to this point, the name Elohim is used. What might account for this change? (Refer to "Background on Yahweh.")

Read Genesis 3:1-7

4. What does the serpent say to the woman?

   What do you think he is trying to accomplish?

5. By what Hebrew name does the serpent refer to God?

   Why might he intentionally avoid using the name LORD?

6. How did Adam and Eve respond after disobeying the LORD?

Read Genesis 3:8-21

7. What actions is God performing in these verses?

8. By what name is God revealed here, and how is this significant?

9. From today's lesson, what has God revealed about Himself to you?

   How does reflecting on this attribute(s) help you in your current circumstances?

Day 2
The LORD, Our Deliverance

BACKGROUND OF THE PASSAGE

Though Moses grew up as the adopted grandson of Pharaoh, he finds himself here exiled from Egypt as a result of his murdering an Egyptian who had mistreated a Hebrew slave. For forty years, seemingly forgotten by God, Moses has served as a shepherd for his father-in-law in the land of Midian.

Read Exodus 3:1-3

10. Who is the angel of the LORD? (Cross-references, concordance, Bible dictionary, or topical Bible may be useful.)

11. What purpose might God have in showing Moses a burning bush that "was not consumed"?

    What might Moses be thinking and feeling here?

12. What has God done to get your attention in the past?

    This week?

Notes

Read Exodus 3:4-10

13. Paraphrase the content of what God told Moses.

14. From what has the LORD delivered you in the past?

From what do you need to seek the LORD's deliverance today?

Deeper Knowledge

THE LORD IS RIGHTEOUS AND HOLY

Define *righteous* and *holy*.

What do the following verses say about the LORD's righteousness or holiness? What other references can you find?

- Genesis 18:25

- Leviticus 19:2

- Psalm 11:7

- Isaiah 6:3

- Daniel 9:14

"This will be written for the generation to come, that a people yet to be created may praise the LORD. For He looked down from His holy height; from heaven the LORD gazed upon the earth, to hear the groaning of the prisoner, to set free those who were doomed to death."
Psalm 102:18-20

DEEPER KNOWLEDGE CONT...

THE LORD IS LOVE

Though God is righteous and holy, God is also love (Cf., 1 John 4:7-21). He particularly reveals this attribute through His plan of redemption for unrighteous man. Where do you see God's love revealed as Deliverer and Redeemer in Scripture? Consider this week's readings, as well as others. (A Bible dictionary or concordance may aid your study.)

Explain the relationship between God's love and His righteousness and holiness.

How is this relationship personally significant?

Day 3

The LORD Will Go with You

Read Exodus 3:11-4:17

15. From Exodus 3 and 4, match Moses' objections to God's commission with God's answer to each of Moses' excuses.

OBJECTION	ANSWER
v. _____ Who am I?	I AM WHO I AM. v. _____
v. _____ What is Your name?	I will help you. v. _____
v. _____ They won't believe me.	I will be with you. v. _____
v. _____ I am not eloquent.	What about Aaron? v. _____
v. _____ Send someone else.	God gives 3 signs. vv. _____

16. Which of Moses' objections have you used when God has called you to serve Him?

How does God respond to your objection(s) in His Word?

17. What do you think God is saying about Himself in Exodus 3:14?

How does this revelation of Himself cause you to love Him more?

18. To what difficult task has God currently called you?

How does today's lesson encourage you to willing obedience?

Day 4
The LORD Is So Much More

Read Exodus 34:5-8

My Name is "I AM"

I was regretting the past and fearing the future.
Suddenly my Lord was speaking:
"My name is I AM."

He paused. I waited.
He continued.
"When you live in the past with its mistakes and regrets, it is hard. I am not there.
My name is not I WAS."

"When you live in the future with its problems and fears, it is hard. My name is not I WILL BE."
"When you live in this moment, it is not hard. I am here.
My name is I AM."

Helen Mallicoat

19. In the chart below:
    A. Identify the verse where you find each given attribute of God.

    B. Record how you have witnessed each attribute of God in your life recently.

    C. Provide an outside Scripture reference that also reveals this characteristic of God.

    D. Add an attribute that God has revealed to you as you've studied "Yahweh" this week.

A. ATTRIBUTE	B. GOD'S REVELATION	C. RELATED SCRIPTURE
Compassionate *Verse*		
Gracious *Verse*		
Slow to anger *Verse*		
Lovingkindness *Verse*		
Truth *Verse*		
Forgiving *Verse*		
Just *Verse*		
D.		

20. Choose one of these attributes and ask God to develop it in your life.

21. What was Moses' response to this revelation of the LORD?

22. While circumstances can lead to disappointment, how has God's revelation of Himself been so much more than you expected?

Day 5
Jesus Is Lord

23. Record what Jesus reveals about Himself in each of the following references. (*Note: In original Greek manuscripts, "He" is omitted.)

    John 1:1

    John 8:24*

    John 8:28*

    John 8:58

    Hebrews 1:3

    Revelation 1:8

24. Keeping the above references in mind, explain the relationship between Jesus and the "I AM" of Exodus 3:14.

25. The following references cite Jesus' seven "I AM" statements. Next to each, indicate who Jesus reveals He is, and what it is He offers you in this revelation of Himself.

SCRIPTURE	"I AM..."	OFFER
John 6:35		
John 8:12		
John 10:7-10		
John 10:11-14		
John 11:25		
John 14:6		
John 15:1, 5		

"...God revealed Himself personally and fully in Jesus Christ. It was Christ who was God from the very beginning, who became flesh, and who took upon Himself our sin that we might take upon ourselves the righteousness of God. Yahweh is the God of the present tense; the God of redemption, the God who has revealed Himself fully in Christ Jesus."[2]

26. Which of Jesus' revelations of Himself is most significant to you?

    Why?

Experiencing Knowledge

God's name "Yahweh" indicates His desire to be your personal God, to deliver you from that which harms you, and to reveal Himself to you in a way that exceeds your greatest expectations.

27. What will you do specifically this week to seek Yahweh, your personal God of the present tense?

    Write your prayer of commitment to Him here.

    How does knowledge of this name of God lead you to put your trust in Him (Psalm 9:10)? What specifically will you do today to demonstrate this trust in Yahweh?

Reflection

Knowing God Through His Names — Lesson Four

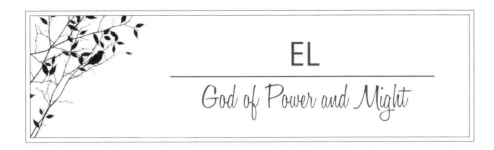

EL
God of Power and Might

In 1969, a little boy played in his backyard as men walked on the moon. Called by his parents, he scampered inside to watch the historical event unfold on the family's black and white TV. Glued to the television screen, he watched every incredible step. Even to this day, he remembers the significance of Armstrong and Aldrin's walk on the moon.

On the other side of the world, Everett Fullam, a missionary in Liberia, tried to explain the extraordinary event that was taking place to Gheo, a tribal chief. The old man looked up at the moon with disgust and disbelief. "There's nobody up there," he countered, measuring the moon between his thumb and index finger. "The moon isn't big enough for two people to stand on." Because Gheo underestimated the moon's size, he missed the magnitude of what was taking place.

In the same way, we often underestimate God, squeezing Him between our own thumb and index finger. Yet, God reveals Himself as El, the God of Power and Might. His display of these attributes throughout Scripture teaches that we can trust Him as El—even in the midst of our seemingly impossible circumstances.

Day 1

Is That Really Laughable?

1. When was the last time you were scared or frightened?

BACKGROUND OF THE PASSAGE

God first promised Abraham a son in Genesis 15:4 when He told Abraham, "...[O]ne who shall come forth from your own body, he shall be your heir." After thirteen long years, Abraham and Sarah still had no baby of their own. In Chapter 18, God returned to reiterate His promise of a child to Abraham and Sarah.

> Read Genesis 18:1-14

2. What was Sarah's response to God's promise? What "logical" reasons could Sarah have given for her response?

3. What did Sarah's response reveal about her opinion of God's power in "impossible" situations?

   What was God's response (verse 14)?

4. The verses below contain words similar to the ones God spoke to Sarah: "Is anything too difficult for the Lord?" Describe the context surrounding the verses listed and what you learn about God's power and might as a result.

PASSAGE	CONTEXT	GOD'S POWER AND MIGHT
Jeremiah 32:17		
Jeremiah 32:27		
Matthew 19:26		
Luke 1:37		

Memory Verse

"...O LORD, the God of our fathers, are You not God in the heavens? And are You not ruler over all the kingdoms of the nations? Power and might are in Your hand so that no one can stand against You."

2 Chronicles 20:6

Over 250 times in the Old Testament, God is referred to as "El," declaring to all generations that power and might are in His hands. Perhaps if Sarah had recognized God as El, she would have been able to respond to God's great promise with joy and praise instead of laughter and doubt. "'El' speaks of God as the great doer and producer. He is the One who exercises such power that whatever is made, done, kept, or destroyed is His doing."[1]

5. Understanding El to be the God of Power and Might, what conclusion should you draw about a seemingly impossible situation that you or someone around you is now facing?

Key Term

El: The God of Power and Might

When used in conjunction with other names of God (e.g., El Elyon—God Most High; El Roi—the God Who Sees; and El Olam—the Everlasting God), "El" lends added emphasis of God's power and might.

Day 2
Jehoshaphat's Impending Tragedy

BACKGROUND OF THE PASSAGE

Jehoshaphat, one of Judah's godly kings, had traveled throughout the region, encouraging the people to seek the Lord wholeheartedly. All was well in the land, not a trouble in sight…until the nation faced impending tragedy. In Jehoshaphat's story, as recorded in 2 Chronicles 20:1-30, we see a vivid example of El revealing Himself as the God of Power and Might.

Read 2 Chronicles 20:1-4

6. What impending tragedy did Jehoshaphat and the people face (verses 1-2)?

7. Why was the situation of such great concern to Jehoshaphat?

8. How did Jehoshaphat react to the threat against his kingdom?

9. What current or past situation has caused you to be fearful?

10. In what ways have your past responses to fearful situations been similar to and/or different from Jehoshaphat's?

Read Lamentations 3:19-26

Both Jeremiah in Lamentations and Jehoshaphat in 2 Chronicles remembered specific times they had seen God's faithfulness in their lives.

11. Jeremiah begins this portion of Scripture by lamenting his difficulties. What is the result?

12. What does Jeremiah do that brings him hope despite his circumstances?

Read 2 Chronicles 20:5-12

13. What attributes and actions does Jehoshaphat recall about God? How does this proper focus influence his response to the impending tragedy?

Notes

14. How does Jehoshaphat's response open the door for God to work?

15. What current situation are you tempted to handle on your own?

16. In what ways do the truths of this passage encourage you to trust God in the middle of your circumstances?

Like Jeremiah and Jehoshaphat, you can draw strength and hope from remembering God's faithful care and intimate involvement in your life. You might consider keeping a "Memory Journal" to chronicle and preserve these testimonies of God's power and might. Start now by listing some specific ways you have seen God work in your life.

Days 3 & 4
God's Powerful Triumph

> Read 2 Chronicles 20:14-19

17. In the chart on the following page, record the specific instructions the Spirit of the Lord gave to Jehoshaphat and the people of Judah. Put an asterisk (*) by repeated instructions. Prayerfully consider how you might apply these instructions to your current circumstances.

Notes

INSTRUCTIONS GIVEN TO JEHOSHAPHAT	APPLICATION TO CURRENT CIRCUMSTANCES

18. What encouragement did the Lord provide along with His instructions?

19. How does this passage encourage you in your circumstances?

20. How did Jehoshaphat and the people respond to the Lord's instructions and encouragement?

Notes

21. Tragedy was still looming; nothing had changed. What motivated Jehoshaphat and the people to respond to God in such a way?

> ### Deeper Knowledge
>
> Review both Hannah's song of praise in 1 Samuel 2:1-10 and Mary's song of praise in Luke 1:46-55. What were the circumstances surrounding each woman's declaration of praise? Record the specific attributes of God they mention. Write your own declaration of praise to the Lord.

22. What practical activities could you do to offer praises to the Lord in the middle of your own difficult circumstances?

Read 2 Chronicles 20:20-30

23. What final instructions does Jehoshaphat give the people as they head into battle?

24. What reaction did the people have to Jehoshaphat's final instructions?

Notes

25. How is God's power and might revealed in the results of the battle?

26. From the text of 2 Chronicles 20:1-30, write the phrase that impacts you most, and explain its significance.

Day 5

My Response to El's Might and Power

27. Compare and contrast Sarah's response to God's promise of a son with Jehoshaphat's response to impending tragedy.

    Similarities:

    Differences:

JESUS, MIGHTY AND STRONG

28. Review the following verses and record the responses that God desires.

    I Peter 5:6-7

    Psalm 18:1-3

    Psalm 37:7

    Psalm 46:10

    Psalm 105:4

Experiencing Knowledge

29. How do your responses to the all-powerful and almighty El compare to the examples in Scripture from this week's study? What steps will you take this week to respond in the way God desires?

30. How does knowledge of this name of God lead you to put your trust in Him (Psalm 9:10)? What specifically will you do today to demonstrate this trust in El?

Reflection

Knowing God Through His Names — Lesson Five

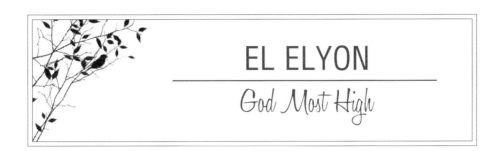

EL ELYON
God Most High

It was not an unfamiliar song that her grandchildren were singing; Mary felt she had known it all her life. As a child, she had belted out the lyrics and even performed them with her hands. Though she had known the simple words all these years, she hadn't really thought about their profound meaning. You, me, brothers, sisters, moon, stars, mommies, and babies…He's got the whole world in His hands.

As she listened to the children sing this precious truth, she sat reflecting on her long life. She had steadily learned to trust God over the years. On this day, He reminded her that He does have the whole world in His hands. Though not always clear in the past, she now recognized the unmistakable evidence of God's guidance and control in her life. She was thankful that sovereign God had given her faith to trust Him. She thanked El Elyon, God Most High.

Today when Mary hears "He's Got the Whole World in His Hands," she is reminded of God's power, His sovereignty, and His ability to take care of His creation. Yes, powerful truth about the one true God is tucked into that simple children's song.

This same truth is reflected in God's name "El Elyon." When revealing Himself as "God Most High" in Scripture, He declares His sovereignty and supremacy. He does have the whole world in His hands.

Day 1
Meeting God Most High

1. If you could have dinner with a powerful or famous person, who would it be and why?

2. Define the following terms:

    Sovereign

    Supreme

3. How do these terms fit with our definition of Elyon to the side?

We first get a glimpse of El Elyon as we study God's covenant with Abram. In Genesis 12:1-3, God first speaks to Abram and declares:

"Go forth from your country, and from your relatives and from your father's house, to the land which I will show you; and I will make you a great nation, and I will bless you, and make your name great; and so you shall be a blessing; and I will bless those who bless you, and the one who curses you I will curse. And in you all the families of the earth shall be blessed."

4. Underline all God's promises to Abram. What was Abram's responsibility?

> Read Genesis 12:4 and Hebrews 11:8

5. What does Abram's response indicate about his relationship with God?

Memory Verse

"I cry out to God Most High, to God, who fulfills His purpose for me."

Psalm 57:2, NIV

Key Term

Elyon comes from the word "alah," which means "to go up" or "highest," indicating the elevation or exaltation of a person or thing. When applied to God, it means that He is "The Exalted One," far above any other god or man.[1]

6. Describe a time when God asked you to step out in obedient faith, even though you did not have full understanding of His purpose.

Notes

What were the results of taking God at His Word?

BACKGROUND OF THE PASSAGE

After Abram relocates his family to the land of Canaan, war breaks out in the region where his nephew Lot has settled; Lot is taken captive, and his possessions are confiscated. Learning of Lot's predicament, Abram pursues and rescues him. (Cf., Genesis 12-14:16)

Read Genesis 14:17-24

7. What do you learn about Melchizedek from this passage and Hebrews 7:1-10?

8. What does Melchizedek say to Abram? By what name does Melchizedek call God?

   In which of your life's circumstances have you seen God reveal Himself to you by this name? (See Key Term)

9. In this passage, how does Abram's response to the king of Sodom (verses 22-24) reveal his confidence in God's covenant from Genesis 12:1-3?

10. What has God promised you in His Word? How do your actions reveal confidence in the surety of His Word as the God Most High?

Day 2
Daniel's God Most High

Daniel was a young Israelite boy taken into captivity by the Babylonians as a result of God's judgment on the nation of Israel. Daniel and his three friends find themselves in the middle of this judgment, where God sovereignly accomplishes His purposes through them.

Read Daniel 2:1-38

11. How does Daniel respond when he hears of the king's plan to kill all his wise men? How would you characterize Daniel based on his response?

12. What is your typical response when circumstances appear to be out of control? How might this response characterize you?

13. Make a list of the ways God reveals His sovereignty in Daniel 2:19-38.

    Why do you think God reveals Himself to King Nebuchadnezzar in these ways?

    Why do you think God has now revealed Himself to you in these ways?

Notes

After Daniel miraculously interprets Nebuchadnezzar's dream, the king honors God and Daniel. Nebuchadnezzar must later relearn the lesson of humility before again acknowledging God as the Most High in Daniel 3:26. In chapter four, Nebuchadnezzar once more fails to "recognize that the Most High is ruler over the realm of mankind" and is given a second dream to be interpreted by Daniel.

Read Daniel 4:24-37

14. Explain why Nebuchadnezzar is driven away to the wilderness.

15. What attitude was hindering Nebuchadnezzar from recognizing that God is Most High? What other attitudes might hinder someone in the same way?

16. What is the king's response to God after his time in the wilderness? List specific words and phrases the king uses to acknowledge that God is indeed the Most High.

Which of these words or phrases echoes the sentiments of your heart as you have studied El Elyon so far? What expressions of praise can you add to the list?

Notes

Day 3

Focusing on God's Sovereignty

17. From the following references, record what you learn about God Most High and how He exercises His supreme rule and care.

    Deuteronomy 32:39

    Job 12:10

    Psalm 36:6

    Proverbs 20:24

    Isaiah 45:6-7

    Mark 4:39

    John 19:10-11

    Acts 17:26

    Philippians 1:6

18. Which specific verses either encourage or challenge you? Explain why.

19. As you reflect on your current circumstances, evaluate how often you are mindful of God's sovereign control in your life. Circle your answer.

    0   1   2   3   4   5   6   7   8   9   10

    Never   Constantly

Read Psalm 57

20. Describe the emotions David might have been feeling as he sat in the cave.

Notes

21. David responds to his difficult circumstances by meditating on truths about God. What are these truths, and what is the result?

22. Describe a time when meditating on God's Word influenced how you viewed your circumstances.

23. List some favorite Scriptures that have been particularly helpful in reshaping your perspective in the past.

24. What specific promise from Scripture will you believe by faith, regardless of how impossible the outcome might seem?

Day 4
Our Response to God's Sovereignty

25. "For the LORD Most High is to be feared, a great King over all the earth" (Psalm 47:2). What attitudes and actions are reflected in a person who appropriately fears the Lord?

    How do your attitudes and actions reflect your fear of the Lord?

It has been said that the longest distance on earth is the eighteen inches from our head to our heart. That is the difference between knowing the truth and really believing it in our hearts. Head knowledge is just information that does not necessarily lead to action. Heart knowledge happens when the truth of God's Word is driven deep into our hearts and changes how we think and act. It happens when we take God at His Word, regardless of how we feel or how bleak the circumstances might appear.

Read Psalm 7:17

26. According to this verse, what actions reflect an understanding of God's supreme care as the Most High? Describe how your life exhibits these actions.

27. What is the most challenging circumstance you are presently facing? How is it affecting your joy?

Read James 1:2-4

28. What is the purpose of trials?

29. How are we to respond to these trials?

30. In what ways does this passage encourage you in the midst of your present hardship?

> It is easy to be thankful and praise God when circumstances are pleasant, but what about when life gets hard?

Read Philippians 4:11-13

31. What had Paul learned as he walked with the Lord?

32. Explain the relationship between contentment and the doctrine of God's sovereignty.

33. Personalize Philippians 4:13 by inserting an area where God is challenging you to be more content: "I can _____ through Him who strengthens me." Tell how you plan to remind yourself of this truth throughout this week.

> "I can do all things through Him who strengthens me."
> Philippians 4:13

Day 5
God's Sovereignty and Our Purpose

Read Ephesians 1:1-14

34. According to this passage, list all God has accomplished for the believer.

35. What ideas are repeated in verses 5, 9 and 11? How are these meaningful to you?

36. How does this passage encourage you to trust El Elyon to accomplish His will in your life?

Read Romans 8:28-30

37. What do these verses reveal about God's desire for His chosen people?

38. How have you seen Him working in your own life to conform you to Christ's image?

Read Galatians 5:16 and Philippians 2:12-13

39. According to these verses, what is a believer's role in the growth process?

40. Explain the relationship between God's sovereignty and a believer's obedience.

41. Knowing that maturity is God's desire for His children, how have you been cooperating with His plans?

Experiencing Knowledge

1 Thessalonians 5:24 tells us, "Faithful is He who calls you, and He also will bring it to pass." What a wonderful cause for confidence in God Most High! Through His supreme power and might, He alone is able to accomplish His desire for our lives.

> "Faithful is He who calls you, and He also will bring it to pass."
> 1 Thessalonians 5:24

42. What is one area that you need to recognize El Elyon's sovereignty in your life? Write out a prayer of commitment to trust him in this situation.

43. How does knowledge of this name of God lead you to put your trust in Him (Psalm 9:10)? What specifically will you do today to demonstrate this trust in El Elyon?

Deeper Knowledge

The Harmony of God's Attributes

When we say that El Elyon is sovereign, we acknowledge that He is the all-powerful, supreme ruler of all. However, sovereignty in the absence of goodness and love results in tyranny. In order to fully appreciate the beautiful masterpiece of God's sovereignty, we should study it in combination with His other attributes.

Use a Bible dictionary, encyclopedia or other Bible resource to identify some of the other attributes of God and His character. Define the terms and use Scripture to support your findings. How does studying these attributes and characteristics increase your understanding and appreciation of God's sovereignty in your life?

Knowing God Through His Names

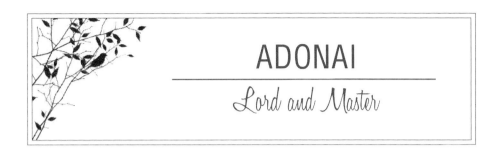

ADONAI
Lord and Master

"Why do you call Me, 'Lord, Lord'? Why do you call me Master...and do not do what I say?" She stood fidgeting during the last hymn—the sound of the music resonating in her ears, as she contemplated what she had just heard.

"All to Jesus, I surrender; all to Him I freely give…." What did that word **all** mean, anyway? She had prayed to receive Christ at 16, but had she surrendered **all** to Him? She could not say yes. "I will ever love and trust Him, in His presence daily live…." Was she trusting and loving Him no matter what? Again, she could not say yes. Life had not been fair in her mind; she had not yet discovered God's unwavering faithfulness and abundant goodness.

"All to Jesus I surrender; humbly at His feet I bow..." She knew in her heart that she was prideful; sadly, it came so naturally.

"Worldly pleasures all forsaken; take me, Jesus, take me now." She sang those last words a bit more forcefully than she had planned. They came as a prayer, as her desire to "surrender all" grew. Such could only be explained as the hand of God working in her troubled heart.

As the song continued, she reached up to wipe her tear-stained cheeks—only now realizing that she had been crying, crying out to her Lord and Master. "All to Jesus, I surrender; Lord, I give myself to Thee..." The realization of her heart's prayer—the desire to surrender all—brought peace and comfort she had never experienced and a hope that she knew would be everlasting. God wanted to be more than her Savior; He wanted her to know Him as Adonai.

Day 1

Adonai: Your Master

1. Reflect on the leaders you have had in life. Describe a boss, teacher, pastor, or parent that you have wanted to please. What about this leader made you want to please him or her?

BACKGROUND OF THE PASSAGE

In Genesis 12-13, God promises Abram descendants, blessings, and land. In Genesis 14, Abram refuses worldly treasure from the king of Sodom, instead trusting the Lord to provide for his needs. The Lord now comes again to Abram in chapter 15.

> Read Genesis 15:1-3

2. What does the Lord say to Abram?

3. The name "Adonai" first appears in Genesis 15:2, when Abram acknowledges the Lord as Master of his life. What does Abram's response reveal about his opinion of his Master?

> Read Genesis 15:4-6 and Romans 4:16-22

4. What two promises does the Lord make to Abram? Find their fulfillment in Scripture.

   Promise:

   Fulfillment:

   Promise:

   Fulfillment:

5. In what ways have you personally experienced God fulfilling promises from His Word?

Memory Verse

"I said to the LORD, 'You are my Lord; I have no good besides You.'"

Psalm 16:2

Adonai is written "Lord" and is different from "LORD" which means Yahweh.

Key Term

Adonai is always translated "Lord." It is distinguished from Jehovah (LORD). "The name *Adonai*, while translated 'Lord,' signifies ownership or mastership and indicates 'the truth that God is the owner of each member of the human family, and that He consequently claims the unrestricted obedience of all.'"[1]

6. From today's reading, what does Abram believe about Adonai?

7. How has today's study influenced your thinking and feelings about Adonai? How does your life reflect this belief?

Day 2
Choose Your Master

What comes to mind when you think about slavery? Modern concepts of slavery are much different than ancient world reality, where such economic practice was commonplace and acceptable. Surprisingly, most slaves at that time received excellent treatment and often fared better than free persons. Even God, in the law of Moses, made special provisions to protect slaves.

> Read Deuteronomy 15:12-18

8. What are God's commands concerning the treatment of slaves? What do they reveal about God's character as a Master?

9. Under what circumstances might a slave commit to permanent servanthood?

   Describe the means by which this slave permanently joined himself to his master. Why do you think the law required such a physically painful act?

Notes

10. What has it cost you to commit to Adonai? What about the Lord makes commitment to Him worth any cost?

Although slavery is not common in today's economic climate, the New Testament reveals that all of us are slaves to a spiritual master. Our decision, therefore, concerns not whether we want to be a slave, but rather who will be our master.

Read Romans 6:6-23

11. What two masters are cited in the text? Give verses and key words or phrases.

    Right master:

    Wrong master:

12. List the consequences and/or blessings received from serving each master.

CONSEQUENCES	BLESSINGS

13. Why do people choose the wrong master? (Use of additional Scripture is encouraged.)

14. Which master have you chosen? What has led you to choose this master? What kind of master has he proven to be?

While kurios can mean any lord or master, when used in the New Testament, it refers primarily to the Lord Jesus. Because all names of God have their full revelation in Jesus Christ, Scripture makes it clear that He is the Master to which we should bow.

Deeper Knowledge

Galatians 5:1 says, "It was for freedom that Christ set us free; therefore keep standing firm and do not be subject again to a yoke of slavery." Explain the concepts of "freedom" and "slavery" in light of today's study. (See also Matthew 11:28-30; John 8:31-44; Romans 8:15; 1 Corinthians 7:22; Hebrews 2:14-15; et al.)

Address the following questions in your response:
- How is freedom from Adonai not really freedom?
- How is slavery to Adonai true freedom?
- What does it mean that Christ has set believers free from slavery?

Day 3
Trust Your Master

Our relationship as a servant to the Lord begins with trust. Adonai keeps His promises and desires our good. We must believe that living under His lordship is better than our independence from Him. We are to trust that He is the right Master.

Read John 20:19-29

15. **Describe the thoughts and emotions of the disciples (including Thomas) before the resurrected Jesus revealed Himself to them. What actions indicate that the disciples thought their Master had let them down?**

    Can you remember a time when you were disappointed with something God allowed in your life? What lesson have you since learned from this experience?

"Preserve my soul, for I am a godly man; O You my God, save Your servant who trusts in You. Be gracious to me, O *Lord, for to You I cry all day long. Make glad the soul of Your servant, for to You, O *Lord, I lift up my soul.
For You, *Lord, are good, and ready to forgive,
and abundant in lovingkindness to all who call upon You. Give ear, O LORD, to my prayer; and give heed to the voice of my supplications!
In the day of my trouble I shall call upon You, for You will answer me.
There is no one like You among the gods, O *Lord,
nor are there any works like Yours.
All nations whom You have made shall come and worship before You, O *Lord, and they shall glorify Your name. For You are great and do wondrous deeds; You alone are God."
Psalm 86:2-10
[*Adonai]

16. What words of Jesus should the disciples have remembered from Matthew 16:21?

    How has recalling truth from God's Word led you to greater trust in Him? What truth do you need to remember now?

The book of Nehemiah depicts the return of the Jews to Jerusalem from Babylonian captivity. Chapters 9 and 10 record the people's repentance and commitment to God.

Read Nehemiah 9

17. In verses 1-3, how did God's people prepare to come before the Lord? How can you relate these preparations to modern day? What one can you do?

18. What attributes of God are revealed in this passage? Make a list as you read through this amazing summary.

19. How do the Lord's actions in this passage attest to His trustworthiness as Master?

20. In the style of Nehemiah 9, write your own history of God's relationship with you.

What attributes of Himself has God revealed to you through His involvement in your life? How has God proven to be a Master worthy of your trust?

Day 4
Surrender to Your Master

Once we trust that the Lord is the right Master, our natural response to Him is surrender. This submission is marked by a willingness to set aside our own desires for Adonai's.

> Read Isaiah 6:1-8

21. From Isaiah's vision, list words and phrases that describe the physical attributes of Adonai and His dwelling place (verses 1-2). How is Isaiah affected by this experience (verse 8)?

22. Why is it significant that Isaiah refers to God as Adonai in verses 1 and 8? How else is God revealed in this passage as Lord and Master? (Consider Key Term from page 2.)

23. Record the Lord's request and Isaiah's response. What is the correlation between how we view God and our willingness to serve Him?

> Once we trust that the Lord is the right Master, our natural response to Him is surrender. This submission is marked by a willingness to set aside our own desires for Adonai's.

24. How does Isaiah's vision motivate you to willingly surrender to Adonai?

JESUS, OUR MASTER

25. As we learned earlier in the study, Jesus is the full revelation of Adonai. Besides revealing Himself as Master, He also modeled perfect surrender to the Father. What do the following references reveal about Jesus' attitude toward total surrender to His Father?

    Mark 14:36

    John 4:34

    John 6:38

    John 14:31

    Philippians 2:5-8

    What lessons do you learn from Jesus' example of surrender?

26. What motivated Jesus' surrender to the Father? (Additional Scripture may be helpful.)

27. In what situation in your life will you now surrender and adopt Jesus' words: "Yet not what I will, but what You will"? Write out your prayer of confession and commitment below.

I Surrender All

All to Jesus, I surrender;
All to Him I freely give;
I will ever love and trust Him,
In His presence daily live.

Refrain:
I surrender all, I surrender all,
All to Thee, my blessed Savior,
I surrender all.

All to Jesus, I surrender;
Humbly at His feet I bow,
Worldly pleasures all forsaken;
Take me, Jesus, take me now.

All to Jesus, I surrender;
Make me, Savior, wholly Thine;
Let me feel the Holy Spirit,
Truly know that thou art mine.

All to Jesus, I surrender;
Lord, I give myself to Thee;
Fill me with Thy love and power;
Let Thy blessing fall on me.

Day 5
Live to Please Your Master

Our knowledge of God as Adonai develops through these steps of faith: (1) Choosing the Lord as the right Master; (2) Recognizing His lordship as trustworthy; and (3) Surrendering to His will over our own. Knowing God as Adonai reaches maturity as we live completely for Him.

> **Read Colossians 1:9-12**

Paul, concerned about the threat of heresy to the church in Colossae, writes to commend their faith, protect their doctrine, and promote their growth in Christ.

28. **What does Paul say is the main purpose of his prayer for the Colossian believers (verse 9)?**

    Verse 10 explains the reason for his request: "...so that you will _____ of the Lord [kurios], to _____ Him in all respects."

29. **In verses 10-12, list the four areas Paul prescribes for walking in a manner that is worthy of and pleasing to the Lord. Explain each in your own words and provide a way one might practically apply each to her own life.**

WALK WORTHY/ PLEASE LORD	PARAPHRASE	PRACTICAL APPLICATION
Bearing fruit in every good work (v. 10a)		
Increasing in the knowledge of God (v. 10b)		
Strengthened with all power (v. 11a)		
Steadfastness and patience; joyously giving thanks (vv. 11b-12)		

Notes

30. In which area have you seen the most growth as you seek to be obedient to your Master?

Read Colossians 1:13-23

31. List all that the Lord has done for believers. How else is He portrayed as Master in this passage?

32. Which of the above observations about Jesus are most meaningful to you, and how do they motivate you to please the Lord?

Experiencing Knowledge

33. How does knowledge of this name of God lead you to put your trust in Him (Psalm 9:10)? What specifically will you do today to demonstrate this trust in Adonai?

My Responsibility

I am glad to think I am not bound to
make the world go right,
but only to discover and to do,
with cheerful heart, the work
that God appoints.

I will trust in Him,
that He can hold His own;
and I will take His will,
above the work He sendeth me,
to be my chiefest good.
The glory is not in the task,
but in the doing it for Him.
Jean Ingelow

Knowing God Through His Names — *Lesson Seven*

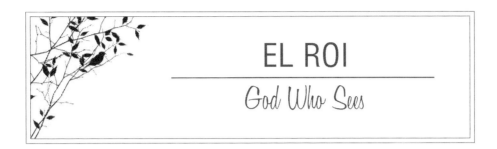

EL ROI
God Who Sees

"WHO PUT A CUCUMBER IN THE TOILET???!!" Of all fascinations, why does the toilet call so loudly to young boys? Is it because it's white and sparkly and clean? Cameron's mom knows who put the cucumber in the toilet. She didn't do it, and it wasn't there this morning when the other kids left for school. "Cameron, did you put the cucumber in the toilet? Cameron, where are you?!"

She doesn't have time for this! She is too stressed by her to-do list: mounting bills; house cleaning and repairs; a job search; phone calls and e-mails to return; and all the little unexpected events that throw her day completely in the wrong direction. She wishes SHE could run and hide!

She discovers Cameron "hiding" with a pillow over his head on the couch. Because HIS eyes are covered, Cameron thinks his mom can't see him. Sure, it's funny, but she doesn't feel like laughing; for suddenly she recognizes that God is teaching her a lesson.

She had been so busy, so blinded by her distractions, that she had forgotten her Heavenly Father sees it all. While she hadn't been looking for Him, He never took His eyes off her. He sees the good, the bad and the funny. God used this produce-in-the-pipe moment to teach—not Cameron, but his mom—that He sees her. He lovingly watches her, knows her heart, and wants to provide relief.

In Genesis 16, we discover another mother, Hagar. She finds herself curled up in a little ball as well, thinking that no one sees her and that no one cares.

Days 1 & 2

Responding to Trouble: Hagar's Plight

1. What type of event would you rather see than just hear about? Why?

God promised Abram and his wife Sarai a son, resulting in descendants too numerous to count. Many years have since passed, but Abram and Sarai are still waiting.

> Read Genesis 16:1-6

2. What trouble are Abram and Sarai having? What solution does Sarai propose to Abram, and what is his response?

3. In what ways is Hagar affected by Abram and Sarai's choices?

4. In what ways have you been affected by the choices of others?

Through no fault of her own, Hagar found herself in the middle of difficult circumstances. John 16:33 declares that "...in the world you WILL have tribulation." Though trials are inevitable, our response is a choice. Hagar chose to run away. God invites us to run to Him.

Jonah and Daniel also find themselves in trouble, as God has called each of them to a difficult task.

5. Complete the chart on the following page with information from the given passages about Jonah and Daniel:
   A. What is each man's assignment?
   B. What is his initial reaction to his trying circumstance?
   C. What is the immediate result of his actions?
   D. What is the ultimate outcome of his circumstance?

Memory Verse

"For the ways of a man are before the eyes of the LORD, and He watches all his paths."

Proverbs 5:21

A. ASSIGNMENT	B. REACTION	C. RESULT	D. OUTCOME
Jonah 1:1-2	Jonah 1:3	Jonah 1:4-17	Jonah 2:10-3:3
Daniel 6:1-9	Daniel 6:10	Daniel 6:11-18	Daniel 6:19-28

6. What insights do you gain from these examples of Jonah and Daniel?

7. Complete the chart below with details of a recent illustration from your own life.

A. ASSIGNMENT	B. REACTION	C. RESULT	D. OUTCOME

8. What lesson do you learn from your experience? How are you like Jonah or Daniel...or both?

Through the examples of Jonah and Daniel, we learn valuable lessons about responding to God in difficult circumstances.

Notes

9. What do the following verses show us that God does for those who run to Him in times of trouble?

   Psalm 32:7

   Psalm 34:17

   Psalm 121

   Psalm 145:18-20

   Nahum 1:7

10. Fill in the blanks from 2 Corinthians 4:16-18.

    Therefore we do not lose heart, but though our outer man is decaying, yet our inner man is being renewed day by day. For momentary, light affliction is producing for us an eternal weight of glory far beyond all comparison, while we _____ not at the things which are _____ , but at the things which are not _____; for the things which are _____ are temporal, but the things which are not _____ are eternal.

11. In what ways do the verses from the previous two questions encourage you to run to God in the middle of your present circumstances?

Day 3

Hagar and the Angel of the Lord

Hagar has run away to escape her difficult circumstances. Discouraged and desperate, Hagar finds herself in the middle of the wilderness, when suddenly the angel of the Lord appears.

Read Genesis 16:7-15

Deeper Knowledge

Who is the angel of the Lord? Record three other examples when the angel of the Lord visited people in the Old Testament. Describe each event and its significance.

12. What instructions and promises does the angel of the Lord give Hagar (verses 9-11)?

13. How might God's instructions and promises have encouraged Hagar to obey God and return to her mistress?

14. Using a commentary or the study notes in your Bible, research the meaning of "Ishmael." Along with your findings, record any insights as to the significance of this name.

15. According to Psalm 40:1-3, what actions did God take when David cried out to Him?

16. Just as God heard Hagar and David, He hears your cries too! How was Psalm 40:1-3 fulfilled in Hagar's life? In your life?

"I waited patiently for the LORD; and He inclined to me and heard my cry. He brought me up out of the pit of destruction, out of the miry clay, and He set my feet upon a rock making my footsteps firm. He put a new song in my mouth, a song of praise to our God; many will see and fear and will trust in the Lord."
Psalm 40:1-3

17. For what have you recently cried out to God? How did God respond to you? What hope has He given you for your future?

Day 4
The God Who Sees

> Read Genesis 16:13-16

18. By what name does Hagar call God? In what ways is this a fitting name for God's revelation of Himself to her?

19. What circumstances of Hagar's life has God seen? Is there anything God hasn't noticed?

> Read Psalm 139

20. Make a list of the things God sees about you (verses 1-6).

21. Make verses 7-10 your own by supplying the places in your life where you need renewed awareness of God's presence.

    Where can I go from Your Spirit?
    Or where can I flee from Your presence?
    If I_____,
    You are there;
    If I_____, behold,
    You are there.
    If I_____,
    If I dwell in_____,
    Even there Your hand will lead me, and Your right hand will lay hold of me.

22. How are you encouraged by the awareness that El Roi sees you?

JESUS WHO SEES

God's ability to see is not limited like ours; He sees completely. God not only sees us in our circumstances, like He did Hagar, but He also sees the condition of our hearts. He knows when we trust Him and when we rely on our sinful selves. We can't hide from El Roi who sees all.

Read 1 John 1:5-10

23. Take a moment to examine your own heart. What sins are you trying to hide from God? What are the consequences of hiding sin?

24. According to the 1 John passage, what remedy for sin does Jesus provide? How does His provision for our sins reveal Him as El Roi?

25. Explain "walk in the Light," and tell how it differs from hiding sins.

26. What are you doing today to "walk in the Light as He Himself is in the Light"? Who is holding you accountable?

Day 5
God Hears and Sees You

Fourteen years have passed. Although God has changed Abram and Sarai's names to Abraham and Sarah, Sarah's heart has not changed; she still despises Hagar.

Read Genesis 21:6-20

27. What demands does Sarah make to Abraham regarding Hagar and her son Ishmael?

"I have a Maker,
He formed my heart.
Before even time began,
my life was in His hand.

He knows my name,
He knows my every thought,
He sees each tear that falls
and hears me when I call.

I have a Father,
He calls me His own.
He'll never leave me,
no matter where I go."
Lyrics and Music by Tommy Walker

28. Describe Hagar's actions and emotions in verses 14-16. What do they reveal about Hagar's trust in the Lord?

29. What question does the angel of God ask Hagar (verse 17)?

30. Once again God sees and hears what is happening in Hagar's life, and He provides everything she needs. How are you trusting God to provide everything you need?

Experiencing Knowledge

31. How has your study of El Roi helped you in at least one specific situation in your life?

32. Summarize each of the passages below. Choose one to write in your own words in the form of a prayer to El Roi.

    Psalm 17:1-3

    Psalm 44:20-21

    Psalm 55:22

    Jeremiah 12:3

33. How does knowledge of this name of God lead you to put your trust in Him (Psalm 9:10)? What specifically will you do today to demonstrate this trust in El Roi?

Reflection

Knowing God Through His Names

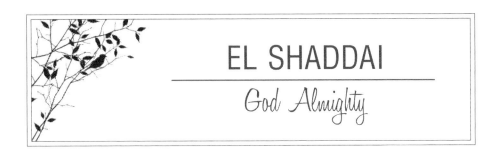

EL SHADDAI
God Almighty

Trish looked out the window and watched the rain pour down. Her heart was heavy. Trish and Dave had been married five years when their troubles began. Dave was deeply invested in the family business and committed to his job. At first, Trish had been impressed with his knowledge about the business and his passion for customer service, but now she found herself increasingly alone as Dave took on more and more customers.

Furthermore, Dave kept postponing their family; he was a planner and wanted everything in order before having a child. With her thirtieth birthday quickly approaching, Trish found herself growing agitated. She was beginning to resent her husband. His business was stealing him away and robbing from her the joy of motherhood.

As Trish continued to look out the window, she could no longer bear her burden. She was tired of this struggle. She fell on her knees and called out to God. As she poured out her heart to her Savior, the words in Matthew came to mind. "Come to me, all who are weary and heavy-laden, and I will give you rest." As she thought about these words, she was reminded that God knew and saw her pain. Trish felt a weight lift from her shoulders; He was carrying her burden for her. Many years ago Trish had come to know Christ as her Savior, but through this struggle she came to know God the Father as her El Shaddai.

El Shaddai is God Almighty. He is the sovereign God Who has the power to fulfill every promise made to His people. He can be trusted to fulfill His Word.

Day 1
Abraham's Almighty God, Fulfiller of Promises

1. Many of us find comfort in a favorite warm drink, pair of sweatpants, food, or place to be. What is one thing that brings you comfort? Why?

BACKGROUND OF THE PASSAGE

Many years ago, God promised Abram land that was beautiful, plentiful, and full of resources. Moreover, this promised land would someday belong to Abram's descendants; God would give Abram an heir, a miracle child from Abram's old body. Twenty-four long years had passed since God had made this promise to Abram. In the meantime, Sarai's maid Hagar bore Abram a son, and strife filled the camp.

At last, God comes and speaks again to Abram: "I am God Almighty." I am El Shaddai, Who is bigger than your age and mightier than human reasoning. Along with these glorious words, God confirms His covenant with Abram and changes his name to Abraham, "Father of a multitude."

> Read Genesis 17:1-2

2. In these verses, what three things does God declare to Abram?

3. Using these declarations and today's Key Term, explain your understanding of God as "El Shaddai."

4. What does God desire from Abram when He says, "walk before Me and be blameless"?

Memory Verse

"He who dwells in the shelter of the Most High will abide in the shadow of the Almighty. I will say to the LORD, 'My refuge and my fortress, my God in whom I trust!'"

Psalm 91:1-2

Key Term

El Shaddai means Almighty God; the sovereign God who is mighty to save, protect, prosper, sustain, and bless.

5. What blessings have you seen in your own life when you've obeyed this command?

Read Genesis 17:1-8

6. In your Bible, mark the promises God makes to Abraham. Why do you think God reveals Himself as El Shaddai in verse 1?

7. What insights or emotions did you experience as you marked these promises? What do you think Abraham's reaction was upon hearing them?

Read Genesis 17:3, 17 and Romans 4:16-21

8. What is Abraham's response to God's promises? What do you learn about Abraham from his response?

> "A Psalm of David. The Lord is my shepherd, I shall not want. He makes me lie down in green pastures; He leads me beside quiet waters. He restores my soul; He guides me in the paths of righteousness for His name's sake. Even though I walk through the valley of the shadow of death, I fear no evil, for You are with me; Your rod and Your staff, they comfort me. You prepare a table before me in the presence of my enemies; You have anointed my head with oil; my cup overflows. Surely goodness and lovingkindness will follow me all the days of my life, and I will dwell in the house of the Lord forever."
> Psalm 23

Day 2

Israel's Almighty God, Powerful Protector and Sustainer

In Exodus chapters 7-13, God fulfills His promise to deliver the children of Israel from the Egyptians. Despite God's powerful acts in Egypt, the Israelites still fail to see God as El Shaddai.

Read Exodus 14

9. Describe the Israelites' reaction to the quickly approaching Egyptians (verses 10-14).

10. Create a timeline of God's powerful acts from Exodus 14. How do the events reveal God as El Shaddai?

11. In Exodus 14:14, what does God require of the Israelites?

"Be still, and know that I am God..."
Psalm 46:10, KJV

Describe a time when God made a similar requirement of you. What was your response to God? Share the outcome.

12. What statements from this passage show God's character as El Shaddai?

13. How could you apply this passage to your current circumstances?

14. If given the opportunity to encourage these Israelites to trust in El Shaddai, to what New Testament passage would you point them? How is this Scripture an encouragement to you today?

Day 3
Job's Almighty God, Who Gives and Takes Away and Gives Again!

Read Job 1

15. What evidence from verses 1-4 shows that God had richly blessed and protected Job as El Shaddai?

16. List the verses and key words found in Job 1 that show Job's reverence of and relationship with God.

17. Supposing you are Job, what are your thoughts and emotions as you read verses 13-19?

18. What is remarkable about Job's reaction to personal tragedy (Job 1:20-22)? What does Job's reaction tell us about his understanding of God as his El Shaddai?

19. Reflect on a time when your manner of dealing with adversity was pleasing to God. What would you say was the key to having this Job-like response?

Notes

Read Job 42

20. Write a simple prayer of worship in response to this chapter and the work of God Almighty in your own life.

Deeper Knowledge

Read Job 39-41

In this passage, God Almighty declares His glorious works. What specific words or phrases direct your heart to worship Him? How might meditating on these chapters help you to worship in the midst of your own difficulties? Make a list of encouraging verses that promote worship in the midst of trial, and share your plan for how you will use it.

Day 4

Paul's Almighty God, Almighty Savior

The ultimate gift which Almighty God bestows on us is salvation. In Acts, we find the amazing account of Paul's transformation from persecutor of Christians to Apostle of Christ. Though not all salvation testimonies are as dramatic as Paul's, every conversion reveals God's power to save and transform!

Read Acts 9:1-22

> "For by grace you have been saved through faith; and that not of yourselves, it is the gift of God; not as a result of works, so that no one may boast."
>
> Ephesians 2:8-9

21. How does this account exhibit Almighty God's power to save? What obstacles were overcome? Whom did God's power affect?

22. What was Paul's response to God's powerful salvation?

    Relate your salvation testimony to Paul's.

> The ultimate gift the Almighty God bestows on us is salvation.

23. How does recounting God's power in your life give you hope for the future?

Read Acts 16:16-34

24. What did preaching the gospel cost Paul and Silas? How is their confidence in Almighty God reflected in their response to their circumstances?

25. In what ways do you see Almighty God at work in this account?

CHARACTERISTICS	EVIDENCE	VERSE(S)
Protecting		
Nourishing		
Sustaining		

26. Reflect on a time when you submitted to God's care and His power was displayed in your life. How did this experience impact those around you?

Day 5
Our Almighty God, Protector and Sustainer

God promises to protect and sustain us. Do we fret and worry, or do we yield ourselves to His almighty care? Psalm 91 speaks of God's response to our need and His powerful protection of those who know and love Him.

> Read Psalm 91:1-2   *Notice four names of God in this passage!

27. Think about the phrase: "dwell in the shelter of the Most High." What do you think it means?

28. Use the following verses to identify benefits or blessings for someone who dwells in the shelter of the Most High.

    Psalm 31:19-20

    Psalm 36:5-9

    Psalm 121

    Isaiah 25:4

29. Describe a time when you "[dwelt] in the shelter of the Most High."

> "Every good thing given and every perfect gift is from above, coming down from the Father of lights, with whom there is no variation or shifting shadow."
> James 1:17

> Read Psalm 91:14-16

30. Make these verses your own by inserting your name and the personal pronoun "her." Write your personalized passage below.

31. What fears do you need to give to Almighty God? How will you respond in thankfulness for His protection?

JESUS, EL SHADDAI

> Read Matthew 6:25-34

These precious truths from Jesus give us great hope that our Almighty God is our Sustainer, the One Who knows and sees our physical needs.

32. Paraphrase the ways Jesus meets our needs.

33. According to verses 31-33, what should be our hearts' focus? What is God's blessing for those who seek what is right?

Experiencing Knowledge

Scripture consistently records God's revelation of Himself as El Shaddai, as we've seen in the lives of Abraham, the Israelites, Job, and Paul. God Almighty fulfills the impossible promise, sustains His people, renews the afflicted, and miraculously transforms even the most resistant sinner. In the same way, our unchanging God desires for us to know Him as El Shaddai, the sovereign God who is mighty to save, protect, prosper, sustain, and bless. As we seek to submit ourselves to His loving care, let's rejoice in the ways in which our Almighty God cares for us!

"Rejoice in the Lord always; again I will say, rejoice! Be anxious for nothing, but in everything by prayer and supplication with thanksgiving let your requests be made known to God. And the peace of God, which surpasses all comprehension, will guard your hearts and your minds in Christ Jesus."
Philippians 4:4; 6-7

Reflection

34. Write a love letter to Almighty God, thanking Him for the way He shows His great power by saving, protecting, sustaining and loving you.

35. How does knowledge of this name of God lead you to put your trust in Him (Psalm 9:10)? What specifically will you do today to demonstrate this trust in El Shaddai?

Knowing God Through His Names

EL OLAM
God Everlasting

Remember the last time you were up to your armpits in housework? The phone wouldn't stop ringing, and your 4 year old "really, really" needed your help. Then the doorbell rang. The sweet girl on the porch offered to de-stress your entire life, if you would just allow her to demonstrate an amazing collection of knives.

These knives last forever; they really do! This pair of scissors can cut through a penny. A real penny! You never have to sharpen them. You never have to buy another knife ever again. This is all you need—unless, of course, you upgrade to the "gracious hostess" collection for an additional $200. Yes, it's expensive, but it lasts forever. "It's money well spent," she assures you. "The penny...remember the penny?"

You bought one amazing knife that day. It's a great knife; at least your tomatoes don't smoosh when you slice them anymore. However, the knife has done nothing to improve your life. Really, what good are these "forever" things if they have no eternal value?

Everyone wants something to last forever: A knife set, an new car, a quality home, furniture, even relationships. Abraham probably felt the same way after being uprooted from his birthplace in Ur. He had been wandering from place to place dwelling in tents (Hebrews 11:9-10). Nothing seemed certain from day to day in Abraham's life...until God revealed himself as El Olam, the Everlasting God.

Day 1
God's Everlasting Faithfulness

1. What earthly possession do you treasure most? Why?

BACKGROUND OF THE PASSAGE

Before Abraham's encounter with Abimelech in Genesis 21, the two men had met once before. Abraham and his beautiful wife Sarah were sojourning in Gerar. Fearing for his life, Abraham lied to King Abimelech, saying that Sarah was his sister. Abimelech then took Sarah into his household. God warned the king in a dream that Sarah was already married; he would die if she was not restored to her husband. Abimelech promptly returned Sarah to Abraham. (Cf., Genesis 20.)

> Read Genesis 21:22-34

2. In verses 22-23, what statements did Abimelech make to Abraham?

   What is the significance of those statements?

3. What was Abraham's complaint, and what was Abimelech's response?

4. Use an outside source such as a commentary or Bible dictionary to research the significance of wells and water at that time. Relate your findings to this passage and to Abraham.

5. How was the conflict resolved?

Memory Verse

"Before the mountains were born or You gave birth to the earth and the world, even from everlasting to everlasting, You are God."

Psalm 90:2

Key Term

Olam: "The Hebrew word Olam expresses the idea of eternal duration; however, it is translated in several different ways in the Old Testament, such as 'ever,' 'everlasting,' 'evermore,' 'forever.'"[1]

6. God was faithful to Abraham by providing water for his family. Where has God been faithful to you?

Day 2

Trusting in God's Everlasting Security

Reread Genesis 21:22-34

7. What actions did Abraham take in response to the covenant?

8. Abraham called God "El Olam," the Everlasting God. Write a definition for Everlasting God. (Hint: use a dictionary to look up "everlasting" and "eternal," and/or look up "Olam" in a concordance or lexicon.)

9. After securing the well and planting a tree, Abraham "calls on the name of the LORD, the Everlasting God." What does Abraham's acknowledgement reveal about his faith?

10. Abraham could have easily placed his confidence in temporal things, such as the well or the treaty he made with Abimelech. Besides the Eternal God, in what do people put their trust today?

Notes

11. What are the characteristics of a person who puts her trust in God's everlasting security? In which of these areas will you ask God to help you grow?

12. How has El Olam provided you with everlasting security?

Day 3

From Everlasting to Everlasting, You Are God

FROM EVERLASTING...

> Read Psalm 90:1-6

Like Abraham, Moses also acknowledged God as everlasting.

13. What could it mean that the Lord is a "dwelling place in all generations"?

14. List phrases from this psalm that show God's relationship to time.

15. Compare this psalm to Genesis 1:1.

16. In what ways is man contrasted with El Olam (verses 3-6)?

...TO EVERLASTING

17. God is not only "from everlasting," but He is "to everlasting." How does Psalm 102:25-28 reflect this truth?

18. Read 2 Corinthians 4:16-5:8. What comparisons does Paul make? How is Paul's mindset shaped by his knowledge that God is "to everlasting"?

19. How does your knowledge of Everlasting God change your attitude toward your circumstances?

Day 4
Trusting in God's Everlasting Strength

Both Abraham and Moses knew God as the Everlasting God. They saw how He provided for them and how He went before them. They relied on His everlasting strength.

"The first thirty-nine chapters of Isaiah set forth the judgments of God upon an iniquitous people. But the opening of chapter forty strikes the keynote for all that follows in the remainder of the book. The succeeding chapters look forward to the time when the nation will have paid sufficiently for her sins."[2]

Read Isaiah 40:28-31 below

²⁸Do you not know? Have you not heard?
   The Everlasting God, the LORD, the Creator of the ends of
   the earth
   Does not become weary or tired.
   His understanding is inscrutable.
²⁹He gives strength to the weary,
   And to him who lacks might He increases power.
³⁰Though youths grow weary and tired,
   And vigorous young men stumble badly,
³¹Yet those who wait for the LORD
   Will gain new strength;
   They will mount up with wings like eagles,
   They will run and not get tired,
   They will walk and not become weary.

Marking the text is a great way to mark basic observations and gain an understanding of what you are reading.

20. Underline all key words (those that are essential or repeated) in the passage above.

21. Contrasts are two opposing ideas or concepts. (Words that indicate contrasts: yet; but; however; although.) Mark contrasts in this passage with ~. Record your findings below.

22. Comparisons indicate similarities or relationships between ideas, concepts, conditions, etc. (Words that indicate comparisons: like; as; also; likewise; just as; so; and.) Mark comparisons with *. Record your findings in the space below.

23. What do these contrasts and comparisons reveal about Everlasting God?

Notes

24. What does it mean to "gain new strength" and "mount up on wings like eagles" (verse 31)?

25. In what ways have you trusted in your own strength during difficult circumstances?

26. Can you remember a time when you trusted in God's everlasting strength during a trial? What was the result?

27. What specific verse from this passage encourages you today?

"Eternal life is not 'endless time,' for even lost people are going to live forever in hell. 'Eternal life' means the very life of God experienced today. It is a quality of life, not a quantity of time. It is the spiritual experience of 'heaven on earth' today. The Christian does not have to die to have this eternal life; he possesses it in Christ today."[3]

Day 5
Eternal Life in Christ

In this week's study, we have learned that God is El Olam, the Everlasting God. The Greek translation for Olam in the New Testament is Aionios, meaning "eternal". Because God is everlasting, He is able to give eternal life to all who believe.

28. What do each of the following verses reveal about eternal life in Christ?

   John 1:1

   John 1:18

   John 12:44-45

   John 17:3

   Romans 10:17

   Hebrews 1:3

29. Based on these references, how would you explain eternal life to an unbelieving friend?

30. How are you experiencing eternal life today?

OUR IDOLS AND THE EVERLASTING GOD
Read Jeremiah 10:1-10. Record specific descriptions of idols as contrasted with El Olam.

IDOLS   EL OLAM

Write a sentence that summarizes Jeremiah's message to Israel.

Rewrite Jeremiah 10:1-10, replacing Israel's idols with examples of contemporary idolatry.

Experiencing Knowledge

Reflection

El Olam is the Eternal God, from everlasting to everlasting. We can trust in His unchanging faithfulness, security, and strength.

31. How does knowledge of this name of God lead you to put your trust in Him (Psalm 9:10)? What specifically will you do today to demonstrate this trust in El Olam?

(E.g., Write down a Scripture verse and post it in a place you will be reminded often; pray each morning that the Holy Spirit will remind you of God as El Olam throughout the day; ask a close friend to keep you accountable for keeping a right perspective; make a list of things you are thankful for as a result of this situation, and post the list where you will see it.)

Knowing God Through His Names

JEHOVAH JIREH
The Lord Will Provide

A well-worn path meandered through the heavily wooded property. Two little girls lived on either side of the lot. They were best friends, and the path had been formed by their countless trips back and forth through the lot to each other's houses.

In the center of the property, amid the towering Monterey Pines, there stood a sprawling oak tree. Much of the young girls' time was spent up in that tree. Seasoned tree-climbers, they would zip high up into its branches in a matter of seconds, their hands and feet having memorized the various routes. Their siblings and other neighborhood children often joined them up in the tree, as there was plenty of room in its welcoming spread of branches. Most often, however, it was the girls' private domain. Sometimes they would sit quietly and discuss the day's events. Other times they would jump and hang and grab, like little monkeys, without fear. The two older brothers of one of the girls attached a rope swing to a sturdy branch, adding a new dimension of thrills for the kids (and a new dimension of anxiety for the parents). In spite of a great deal of time and activity spent in the oak, no serious mishap ever occurred.

Often, the two friends would have a Friday night sleepover at one house or the other. Early one Saturday morning, following a sleepover, the girls were suddenly awakened by a loud, incessant drone. Looking out the window to find the source, they were horrified to see their mighty oak being felled by a chain saw! Little had they known that their time up in its branches the day before would actually be their last time. That day they learned a little bit about life's inevitable losses and disappointments.

Subsequently, many of the trees were cleared, and a beautiful home was built among the remaining oaks and pines. As the girls were growing up, they often spoke of that fateful morning and their resultant loss.

To some extent, that must be how Abraham felt when God asked him to give up what he had so long been waiting for. But God revealed Himself to Abraham as Jehovah Jireh, The Lord Will Provide. The resulting changes in his life were dynamic.

Day 1

Abraham's Test

1. When have you experienced the unexpected loss of something important to you?

2. Read Genesis 22:1-19, and give a brief overview of the passage.

3. Abraham was *tested* by God. What reasons does God give for testing His children in the following verses?

   Genesis 22:12

   Exodus 16:4

   Exodus 20:20

   Deuteronomy 8:2

   Deuteronomy 8:16

There is no mention in the narrative of the thoughts and emotions of either Abraham or Isaac. We read in verse 2 only God's directive to "go," "take," and "sacrifice." His obedience appears to be immediate and unconditional.

4. Read Genesis 12:4 and 21:14. Compare Abraham's response in Genesis 22:3 to that of the two former instances. What do his actions indicate about his character?

Memory Verse

"And my God will supply all your needs according to His riches in glory in Christ Jesus."

Philippians 4:19

From today's passage, list the steps of preparation and obedience you see in his response to God's instructions.

How can you apply similar steps in your own life on a daily basis?

> ## Deeper Knowledge
>
> Isaac was to be offered as a burnt offering, which was always a voluntary offering...an offering of love. Read Leviticus 1 and all the footnotes included in your Bible.
>
> List the steps required to offer a burnt offering sacrifice.
>
> By examining your Bible's footnotes and cross references, explain the symbolism found in verse 4.

5. Genesis 22:4 indicates that it was a three-day journey to the land of Moriah where God had instructed Abraham to offer Isaac as a sacrifice. Think of a time when your faith was tested over an extended period of time. How did it affect your relationship with the Lord?

Notes

Day 2
The Lord Will Provide

6. What evidence of Abraham's faith is revealed in Genesis 22:5?

7. Read Genesis 22:12 and Hebrews 11:17-19. What do these verses reveal about Abraham's faith and expectations?

8. What do you think his faith was based on?

9. What is your faith in God based on?

10. Abraham expressed faith that there would be provision before it was provided. What similarities do you see in John 6:10-11?

11. Have you ever felt that God was asking you to do something of unimaginable magnitude? If so, how did you respond? If not, what do you suppose your response would be?

12. God stopped Abraham from killing Isaac because He knew Abraham feared Him. Read Proverbs 1:7 and Ecclesiastes 12:13. Find other verses from cross references or a concordance, and explain what it means to fear God.

Notes

Genesis 22:8 does not imply that Abraham had any foreknowledge of the outcome of his situation, as that would negate the trial of faith. He had responded to Isaac, "God will provide for Himself the lamb for the burnt offering…" Verse 13 records the fulfillment of that statement of faith. Abraham is surprised, as indicated by the word "behold," at the appearance of a ram in the brush.

13. **What was Abraham's action following the appearance of the ram in Genesis 22:13?**

14. **God had provided a ram rather than a lamb that both Abraham and Isaac had referred to. Share when God has provided for you in a way that was different from how you had asked or expected.**

    What did you learn from the experience?

Day 3
Jesus, Our Provision

With what joy, relief, and praise Abraham must have uttered, "The LORD Will Provide": Jehovah Jireh! Literally, it means "to see." The Father sees. It goes with **who** He is. He "sees to it." In verse 8, "God will provide for Himself the lamb…" was essentially, "the Lord will see to it." God would foresee the outcome. He would prearrange it. Here God's providence, His "pro-vision" is revealed.

15. **Using a dictionary, find and write the definitions of the following words:**

    Provide -

    Providence -

    Provision -

"The next day he saw Jesus coming to him and said, 'Behold, the Lamb of God who takes away the sin of the world!'"
John 1:29

16. Read Psalm 31:14-15 and Romans 8:28. How does your awareness of God's providential watch care, His pro-vision, impact you in your Christian walk?

    When faced with pressing issues, can you with faith say, "The Lord will see to it"? What circumstances will you turn over to Him today?

The ram was a complete provision of a substitute in place of Isaac. This is the first appearance in Scripture of a substitutionary sacrifice, for Abraham offered up the ram "in the place of his son."

17. Read Hebrews 10:1-10 and compare and contrast the Old Testament sacrifices with Christ as a sacrifice. What is the result of Christ's sacrifice?

18. Read Mark 10:45, Hebrews 2:17, and 1 John 2:2. Using your Bible footnotes or Bible dictionary, define ransom, propitiation and atonement (NIV). Record your findings.

19. Read Genesis 22:16 and Romans 8:32. What similarities do you see between these two verses?

    Reread Romans 8:32 out loud, and replace "us all" and "us" with your name. Thank God for His provision.

> "The Son is the radiance of God's glory and the exact representation of His being, sustaining all things by His powerful word. After He had provided purification for sins, He sat down at the right hand of the Majesty in heaven."
>
> Hebrews 1:3, NIV

In 2 Corinthians 9, Paul summarizes a section on giving; praising God for the best Gift ever given!

20. Read 2 Corinthians 9:15. How would you describe God's "indescribable gift" and what does it mean to you personally?

Days 4 & 5
Trust and Obey

Abraham and Isaac's emotional responses are not recorded in the Genesis 22 event. We can only surmise that their hearts were lighter on their return trek than on their initial three-day journey. The Israelites had a forty year journey to deal with.

21. Read Exodus 6:6-8. What promises did God make to the Israelites while they were still suffering in Egypt?

> We can only surmise that their hearts were lighter on their return trek than on their initial three-day journey.

22. God's providential care was evident to the Israelites prior to their exodus from Egypt. Fill in the chart to highlight God's watch care.

VERSES	EVENT	GOD'S PROVIDENCE
Exodus 8:20-23		
Exodus 9:1-7		
Exodus 9:22-26		
Exodus 10:21-23		
Exodus 12:35-36		

23. What do the following references reveal about how God provided for the Israelites during their time in the wilderness?

    Deuteronomy 8:1-4

    Deuteronomy 29:5-6

    Psalm 105:37

24. Choose one of the following Scriptures and use it to summarize the often-negative attitude the Israelites displayed, in spite of God's care.

    Exodus 15:22-24

    Exodus 16:2-3

    Exodus 17:1-7

    Numbers 11:1-6

25. What do you grumble about when you get tired of God's provision? Right now, prayerfully consider what He may be teaching you through current difficulties.

26. Read Deuteronomy 8:17-18, Isaiah 31:1, and Daniel 5:1-4, 23. What do these verses reveal about misplaced praise, glory, and trust?

27. Identify some ways that people try to provide for themselves today.

28. Scripture instructs us on how we are to utilize our earthly possessions and gifts that God has provided. What do you find in the following verses?

    1 Timothy 6:17-19

    James 1:17

    1 Peter 4:10-11

Experiencing Knowledge

29. Prayerfully examine your attitude regarding your material possessions and God-given talents. Is there anything you are holding back from God?

30. Many of God's provisions are not tangible. Read and meditate on Psalm 104. Select three of God's providential blessings recorded in this psalm and share why they are meaningful to you.

31. What provisions, tangible and intangible, that are not included in this psalm are you most thankful for? Thank God now for these blessings.

32. How does knowledge of this name of God lead you to put your trust in Him (Psalm 9:10)? What specifically will you do today to demonstrate this trust in Jehovah Jireh?

Reflection

Knowing God Through His Names

EL BETHEL
God Our Home

The small white church was still there. It was bright and welcoming, pristinely manicured, in the middle of the one-light town. As Allison pulled into the familiar gravel parking lot, memories raced through her mind. This was where she had given her life to Christ as a teenager. She still wasn't sure why she had made such a huge effort to travel back here.

Growing up on a farm hadn't appealed to Allie. She loved her parents, but didn't appreciate their work ethic. She didn't share their gratitude for what they had, or agree that it was God who had provided it. Even in extra-rural Middle America, Allie had managed to spiral out of control. And even when she couldn't get her hands on some drugs or alcohol, a rebellious spirit ruled her heart.

One person had always been able to momentarily tame Allie. She loved the pastor's wife, Sadie. She was a little older than Allie's parents, and so mild-mannered and compassionate, but had a knowing look in her eyes. Allie knew she had her pegged and she loved her anyway. Sadie was at the church one day when Allie's mother had sent her to deliver homemade jam to the pastor. She invited Allie to help her paint a door and they talked about Allie's life. She identified so much with this woman who was so different from her and she wanted to be like her. Sadie clarified, "Allison, that means being more like Christ. That's the only difference between you and me." In that moment, Allie saw everything so clearly. She grew up in this place, but had never received the truth. She accepted Christ as her Savior, paint in her hair, and her life was never the same. She began to honor her parents and serve the Lord with deep passion.

Allison's parents were gone now and she had no family in town. But God was here. He didn't live in this church, but He had certainly been at work all along and especially the day He had called her to Him. As she walked into Sadie's memorial service, she was overwhelmed with gratitude for the woman who had shown her that God is good and He is here, working. She left a small paintbrush on the coffin before quietly filing out. Even as she drove away, she could not take her eyes off the tiny white building in her rearview mirror. It would always sparkle in her memory.

The small white church is the place where Allison made a commitment to the Lord. When she thinks of that place, she remembers what the Lord has done. People of the Old Testament often identified a place where God had done or was going to do great things. In the story of Jacob, we see God make a promise to Jacob at Bethel, and later God identifies Himself as El Bethel. How will Jacob respond to the One who gave him that promise? Will he himself finally recognize El Bethel?

Day 1

Trusting in God's Promises

1. What is one place (grandma's, a vacation spot, camping place, etc.) that you enjoy returning to each year?

   What special memory do you have there?

BACKGROUND OF THE PASSAGE

Remember the promise that God made to Abraham? God promised Abraham that He would make his name great, and that He would bless those who bless him. After years of moving, God finally gave him a son with his wife, Sarah, secured a well for water and a place for Abraham to stay. Abraham identified God as El Olam, the Everlasting God. Isaac had twin sons, Esau and Jacob. Esau was the first born, which should have provided him the birthright and a double share of the inheritance. However, he bartered his birthright away to Jacob (Genesis 25:31). In this lesson we meet Jacob fleeing his country because of his angry brother and need for a wife. He was headed off to the land of Paddan-aram to his meet his uncle.

> Read Genesis 28:10-22

2. On his way to find a wife, Jacob had a dream. What promises did God make to Jacob (13-15)?

3. Read Genesis 12:1-3 and 26:2-5. What was similar about these covenants, and to whom were they made?

Memory Verse

"...being confident of this, that He who began a good work in you will carry it on to completion until the day of Christ Jesus."

Philippians 1:6, NIV

4. Compare Genesis 28:15 and Philippians 1:6. How is this promise similar to the Genesis passage?

How does this encourage you?

5. What reactions did Jacob have to the dream (16-19)?

What emotions was he feeling?

6. Jacob called the place Bethel, acknowledging that God was there, and made a vow. When was the first time you recognized God's presence and knew He was calling you to Him?

7. Contrast God's promise to Jacob from your answers in question two with the conditions in Jacob's vow (verses 20-21).

Key Term

Bethel means house of God.

8. What did you learn about Jacob's faith?

What might be a better response?

Have you been giving God stipulations for your obedience? In what areas?

Day 2
God Leads Through His Word

Jacob journeys on after his one night stay at Bethel. He comes to the land of the "sons of the east" (Genesis 29:1). Here he finds his Uncle Laban and meets his daughters, Rachel and Leah. Jacob agrees to work seven years for Rachel's hand in marriage, but after seven years is given Leah instead. Jacob must work another seven years for Rachel. Despite Laban's deception, God fulfills His promise to bless Jacob, and gives him a total of 11 sons and a daughter by his wives and their servants (Genesis 29 and 30). God also continues to bless Jacob with possessions. "So the man became exceedingly prosperous, and had large flocks and female and male servants and camels and donkeys" (Genesis 30:43). Yet, after 14 years of working for Laban's household, Jacob felt it was time to return home. Jacob's children were surrounded with a culture that wasn't honoring God. However, Uncle Laban wasn't so sure they should leave. He liked the way the Lord was blessing Jacob's work with his sheep (Genesis 30:27), and struck a deal with Jacob that if he stayed, Laban would give him a portion of the sheep. God blessed Jacob again with a portion larger than Uncle Laban's, which made Laban's sons angry.

Read Genesis 31:1-13

Notes

9. What circumstances made Jacob feel it was finally time to leave (1-13)?

10. Jacob recognized God's provision in this situation. List the ways God provided.

11. Read Philippians 4:19. In what areas of need does this passage promise that God will provide?

12. God calls Himself the "God of Bethel" in verse 13. What is He reminding Jacob of?

13. Why is it good to recall times or places where God did great works, or met our needs in wonderful ways?

    Recall a time in your life that you have been thankful for what God has done.

Key Term

El Bethel means God of the house of God.

14. Jocob spent a total of twenty years working for dishonest Laban. The circumstances around him were getting tougher. And now God leads Jacob through His Word by saying, "Leave this land and return to the land of your birth" (Genesis 31:13). Today we have God's written Word to direct us. Briefly note the benefit of God's Word found in each verse below.

VERSE	BENEFIT
John 8:31-32	
Romans 10:17	
2 Timothy 3:16-17	
Hebrews 4:12	
James 1:22-25	

15. Recall a situation where God's Word directed you. What happened?

Day 3
The Struggle for Full Obedience

Read Genesis 31:14-21

16. What is Rachel and Leah's response to their husband telling them to move (verses 14-16)?

17. List the family's actions as they prepared to leave (verses 17-21).

18. Re-read Genesis 31:3. What is God's promise in this verse?

    What facts reveal that Jacob still wasn't completely trusting in the Lord?

19. What consequences might happen as a result of Rachel's actions (verses 19, 32)?

20. When God asks for obedience, why is there a struggle to do it our way?

21. Is there an area in your life where you are not fully obeying God?

Read Genesis 31:22-55

22. In what ways do we see God's promise of protection play out for Jacob's family?

    What resulted?

Notes

Day 4
Jacob's Continual Struggles

Skim Genesis 32-34

23. Make notes of the significant events in these chapters.

24. What consequences did Jacob's family deal with in chapter 34:30-31?

THE WAY BACK

Thirty years have passed since Jacob vowed his return to Bethel, and it may have been ten years since leaving Laban. Jacob had built a house in Shechem and lived there.

Read Genesis 35:1-7

LEAVE IT BEHIND

26. What was God's command?

Notes

What did Jacob tell his family to leave behind?

Why would it be important to leave these things before moving?

Is there something in your life that you must leave behind in order to make a change?

Is there something you must bury (materialism, thoughts, pride, sensuality)?

Read Ephesians 4:22-24; Hebrews 12:1-3; 1 Peter 1:13-16. How are we to leave things behind?

Day 5

Back to Bethel

> Re-read Genesis 35:1-7

MAKE A MOVE

27. List the details of the departure (verses 2-4).

What was evidence, once again, of God's promise that He would be with them (verses 5-6)?

Read Genesis 35:9-15

FULL OBEDIENCE LEADS TO WORSHIP

28. When Jacob obeyed and went back to Bethel, God appeared to him again. What was included in this new blessing from God?

29. What was Jacob's response to the blessing?

30. What can we learn from these verses about El Bethel?

    How about Jacob's response?

Deeper Knowledge

In Genesis 35:13-15, a drink offering was poured out to God after Jacob heard the blessing.

Paul used the term in the New Testament in Philippians 2:17 and 2 Timothy 4:6. What is the drink offering a symbol of?

How is this relevant to your life today?

Experiencing Knowledge

Reflection

There was a man living on the streets. He had grown up in a wealthy family but became estranged and hadn't seen his family for eighteen years. He was broken in spirit and had taken to a life of begging. One day he got out at the Pennsylvania depot to begin begging. He touched the shoulder of a man and said, "Hey mister, can you give me a dime?" As soon as he saw his face he realized it was his own father. He said, "Father, do you know me?" His father threw his arms around him, and with tears in his eyes, said, "Oh son, at last I've found you. I've found you. You want a dime? Everything I have is yours."[1]

Our Father waits for us to come back to Him every time we disobey. When we have turned, or returned back, we can receive what He is pleased to give us.

31. Are there things in your life you need to get rid of in order to obey? Are you making a move, on your way back to El Bethel? Can you worship Him knowing you are in obedience to Him? Write your reflections here.

32. Jacob set up a pillar as a reminder of God's promises. What will you do to remind yourself of what you've learned this week?

33. How does knowledge of this name of God lead you to put your trust in Him (Psalm 9:10)? What specifically will you do today to demonstrate this trust in El Bethel?

Knowing God Through His Names — Lesson Twelve

JEHOVAH ROPHE
The Lord Heals

Cancer takes the lives of approximately 1500 people each day. Represented in each of those lives is a story of someone's mom or dad, son or daughter, brother or sister, aunt or uncle, grandparent, cousin, friend. They touch countless others as they go through their own personal struggle and fight against this pervasive and devastating disease.

One such story was Anna's. After a time of remission, she began to suffer symptoms again, and soon test results showed the spread of cancer to her colon, kidneys, and lungs. Cancer was ravaging her body, hope was waning, and there was little left to fight with. In the final days of her life, Anna's sister shared with her the only hope she had. It was not a hope for physical healing, but a lasting hope in The Healer. She shared that Christ died for our sins, and all Anna had to do was accept His payment for her sins through His death, burial and resurrection and she would go into eternity with Jesus. Anna eventually died of cancer, and though she was never healed physically, she did surrender to Jesus in the final days of her life. The believers around her were able to rejoice in spite of their grief. While her physical body was left unhealed, God healed her soul. Today Anna lives as she never did while she was on this earth. She is free from pain, the scars of sin, and alive in the presence of her Savior, her Healer, and God--Jehovah Rophe!

Day 1
God the Healer

1. Do you know of a story similar to Anna's? How has that person's story impacted your own faith?

BACKGROUND ON THE PASSAGE

The people of Israel spent many years under great oppression. From sunrise to sunset, they labored hard in the hot sun making bricks for the Egyptians in the field. It was rigorous work. The pharaohs instructed taskmasters to be ruthless; beatings and whippings occurred on a regular basis. The Israelites were in great need of a savior; a savior who could heal them physically, spiritually, and emotionally. God provided Moses to champion the redemption of the people from slavery, but Pharaoh was not willing to let them go. They watched as God sent many plagues to sway the heart and intentions of Pharaoh, but his heart remained hardened (for further detail, see Exodus 4-11). While the Egyptians suffered through plague after plague, the Israelites did not find themselves completely exempt. It was not until after God took the firstborn son of every family who did not follow the Passover, that He provided the timing and protection for Moses to lead them away from slavery to freedom and the Promised Land. Beyond the Exodus and through the miraculous crossing of the Red Sea, the children of Israel find themselves in the middle of the desert where God reveals Himself as Jehovah Rophe, the Lord who heals.

THE PEOPLE'S PROBLEM

> Read Exodus 15:19-21

2. What miracle did God perform for the Israelites?

3. In what ways did they react (verses 20-21)?

Memory Verse

"Then they cried out to the LORD in their trouble; He saved them out of their distresses. He sent His word and healed them, and delivered them from their destructions."

Psalm 107:19-20

4. What events have caused you to sing praises to God recently?

5. At this point in their journey, what do God's people know about Him? (Hint: Skim back through Exodus 7-15).

Key Term

Rophe (also translated rophi, rohpe, rapha) means to heal, a restoring to normal, an act which God typically performs.

raw-faw' - to mend by stitching, to cure or heal

THE PEOPLE'S RESPONSE

Read Exodus 15:22-27

6. Describe the scene in verse 22.

7. When they came to Marah, what was the problem?

What responses did God's people have (verses 23-24)?

The word Rophe is used about sixty times in the Old Testament. Some of the meanings are: physician, take care of, to heal, purify, or repair.

8. What would you expect from God if you were in their sandals?

9. When you are faced with a difficult situation, how do your reactions compare with the Israelites'?

   What would your best friend say? (Go ahead, ask!)

Day 2
Water to Live By

> Reread Exodus 15:22-27

10. What actions did Moses take (verse 25)?

11. How was Moses' response different than the people's response?

12. How did God provide?

13. Describe a time when you responded more like Moses.

14. What commands does the Lord give the Israelites after providing the sweet water (verse 26)?

Notes

15. What promise does He make to His people (verse 26)?

16. What did this promise specifically mean to the Israelites?

    What does it mean to you today?

17. Look at the Key Term on page 3. Why is it significant that God chose to reveal Himself as Jehovah Rophe at this specific time?

18. Soon after, they travel on to Elim, which is 7 miles from Marah. What was provided there (verse 27)?

    Why didn't God lead them there first?

When we are obedient and walking faithfully with the LORD, He blesses us. These blessings are not always seen when we encounter situations like the bitter waters of Marah. Life difficulties are not what we would expect to receive. God will not always lead us straight to Elim. But He always has in mind to use the bitter waters we encounter, and make them sweet in His time and overall purpose for our lives. We can rest, knowing that He will restore what was once broken in His perfect time.

19. What are the bitter waters you are facing right now or have faced in the past (physically, spiritually, emotionally)? Describe your response.

Notes

Day 3
The Great Physician Heals

20. Read the verses and fill in the chart below.

VERSE	TYPE OF HEALING	WHAT YOU LEARNED ABOUT HEALING
Deuteronomy 32:39		
2 Kings 2:19-22		
2 Chronicles 7:14		
Psalm 30:2		
Psalm 41:4		
Psalm 147:3		
Jeremiah 3:22		
Jeremiah 30:3-4, 17		
Revelation 22:2		

21. Explain the ways Jehovah Rophe heals.

22. What does this show you about Jehovah Rophe?

23. List a few ways God has healed you (do not just consider physical healing).

24. Write a praise to the Lord because He is your Jehovah Rophe.

Day 4
Jesus, Others, and You

The acts of physical healing Jesus performed in the New Testament were designed to help prove the Gospel. In addition to becoming physically healed, people would believe in Jesus and become spiritually and emotionally healed. God's greatest act of healing came as a result of Jesus dying on the cross for our sins; His death, burial and resurrection.

Read Mark 5:21-43

25. What actions did the woman take to become healed?

26. List the ways she was healed.

27. Name the steps the father took to help his daughter.

   Why did he take such risks?

28. Describe the scene as the girl was healed.

29. What is significant about the faith of these two individuals?

Notes

The acts of physical healing Jesus performed in the New Testament were designed to help prove the Gospel.

Deeper Knowledge

Find three more examples of Jesus healing in the New Testament.

VERSE	WHO WAS HEALED?	IN WHAT WAY?	DESCRIBE THE RESULT

30. Read 1 Peter 2:24. How were we healed and what were we healed of (what was our sickness or disease)?

31. What does the word "healed" mean in this context (cf. Matthew 13:15; John 12:40)? (Hint: You may want to consult a commentary or Bible dictionary for help.)

32. Of the types of healing, which is most important and why? Which is guaranteed?

    How do our prayers reflect this?

> "...and He Himself bore our sins in His body on the cross, so that we might die to sin and live to righteousness; for by His wounds you were healed."
> 1 Peter 2:24

33. Look again at 1 Peter 2:24. Reflect on what Jesus did for you and respond with a humble prayer of thankfulness. Tell Him anew of your desire to die to sin and live for righteousness.

Day 5

To Heal or Not to Heal

There was a unique period in history (the time of Christ and the apostles) where healing was a significant part of spreading the gospel. "The command to heal the sick or raise the dead is not found in any of the Epistles written after Calvary. While healing is associated with the gospel of the kingdom, it is not so related with the gospel of the grace of God. Healing is mentioned in several places in the Epistles, but where bodily healing was in view, it is left as an individual matter. God is still *Jehovah-rapha*, but He does not always heal ... He might not heal you or me. But He is able, if He wills to do so. He is still *Jehovah-rapha*. Each child of God must wait upon His heavenly Father for himself in the time of sickness."[1]

Read 2 Corinthians 12:1-10

34. Who is this passage about and what are some things you know about him?

    How does he respond to his "thorn in the flesh" (verse 8)?

    Did God choose to heal? What were the reasons?

    What was Paul's response to God's answer?

    How can you respond more like him regarding your "thorn in the flesh"?

35. What hope do the following verses give you for ultimate healing?

   2 Corinthians 5:16-17

   1 Corinthians 15:42-58

   Revelation 21:1-5

Experiencing Knowledge

36. Is there an area of your life in which you don't feel healed? To what promise can you cling?

37. What can you do this week to use this lesson to encourage someone you know who is hurting right now?

38. How does knowledge of this name of God lead you to put your trust in Him (Psalm 9:10)? What specifically will you do today to demonstrate this trust in Jehovah Rophe?

Reflection

Knowing God Through His Names — Lesson Thirteen

JEHOVAH NISSI
The Lord My Banner

In May 1940, the German Army captured France, causing the retreat of nearly 400,000 Allied soldiers to Dunkirk, a small French city along the English Channel. The destruction of nearby ports prevented Allied ships from rescuing the trapped soldiers. Just fifteen miles separated them from German tanks intent on their extermination; it looked like certain death.

Winston Churchill believed that survival of even 20,000 soldiers would be a miracle. In desperation, King George declared May 26, 1940, a national day of prayer. Entering Westminster Cathedral, Parliament, the Prime Minister, and King lay prostrate before the Lord, crying out to Almighty God for hope and deliverance.

Unknowingly cooperating with Divine sovereignty, Hitler, victory in hand, rejected the advice of his generals and illogically withdrew the German tanks' advancement on Dunkirk. Instead, he ordered the German Air Force to defeat the stranded soldiers.

The very next day, a dense fog suddenly rolled across and covered the entire English Channel. It was not the season for fog; never in recorded history had fog covered the channel in May. Obscured from the German Air Force under this heavy fog, 600 small boats traveled back and forth across the channel for several days, transporting troops to safety. As a result, 338,000 soldiers were saved. Churchill hailed this event a miracle of deliverance, proclaiming, "A guiding hand interfered to make sure the Allied forces were not annihilated at Dunkirk."

It was not the size of England's army that protected her in World War II. England did not rally around her own superior strategy, bravery, or persistence. Having nowhere else to turn, she recognized her only hope was in the sovereign hand of God. Responding to the prayer of faith, the petition for His deliverance, God revealed Himself to England as Jehovah Nissi, the Lord My Banner.

In Exodus 17, the children of Israel, desperate as the soldiers at Dunkirk, find themselves in a similarly hopeless predicament. How will God respond when His people seek Him as their rallying point?

Day 1
Israel's Sin

1. What is one "God-sized" problem you have encountered in your life?

BACKGROUND ON THE PASSAGE

A few weeks prior to the opening scene in Exodus 17, the children of Israel experienced God's sweetening of the bitter waters of Marah. In the wilderness of Sin, their grumbling about the lack of food precipitated God's miracle of manna. Now in Rephidim, the setting for God's revelation of Himself as Jehovah Nissi, the Israelites are once again finding contentment as non-existent as water in the desert.

> Read Exodus 17:1-7

2. What problem do the Israelites encounter in Rephidim, and what complaints do they bring before Moses?

3. How was their "quarreling" putting the Lord to the test?

4. In what ways can you compare yourself to Moses and/or the Israelites in this passage?

Memory Verse

"But thanks be to God, who always leads us in triumph in Christ, and manifests through us the sweet aroma of the knowledge of Him in every place."

2 Corinthians 2:14

5. The rock and water are spiritual symbols. Put the following references under the appropriate heading: 2 Samuel 22:47; Psalm 18:2; Isaiah 26:4; Isaiah 44:8; John 4:1-14; John 7:37-38; I Corinthians 10:4; Revelation 22:17.

   ROCK   WATER

   Explain the symbolism of "rock" and "water."

6. How is the presence of the "rock" and "water" evident in your life?

7. In verse 7, the Israelites unwisely tested the Lord by doubting His goodness and questioning His presence with them. How has the LORD shown that He is with you this week?

   How will you thank Him?

Day 2

God Reveals Himself as Jehovah Nissi

BACKGROUND OF THE PASSAGE

In all of Scripture, Jehovah Nissi ("the Lord My Banner") is found only in Exodus 17:15. After Amalek's defeat at Rephidim, Moses names his commemorative altar Jehovah Nissi, giving full credit and glory to God for Israel's victory.

Key Term

Banner: "A banner, in ancient times, was not necessarily a flag such as we use nowadays. Often it was a bare pole with a bright shining ornament which glittered in the sun. The word here for banner means to glisten, among other things. It is translated variously pole, ensign, standard, and among the Jews it is also a word for miracle. As an ensign or standard it was a signal to God's people to rally to Him. It stood for His cause, His battle. It was a sign of deliverance, of salvation...."[1]

Read Exodus 17:8-16

8. Who were the Amalekites? (Use cross-references and/or concordance.)

9. What was Joshua's role in the battle? What was Moses' role?

10. Which role do you think was more important? Explain your answer.

11. How do you personally identify with Joshua and/or Moses?

12. From verse 14, what did the LORD want Moses to write, and what do you think was His purpose?

13. What events in your life that reveal God's protection and deliverance could you similarly record?

14. How are you passing along your testimonies of Jehovah Nissi to those who will follow after you?

What more could you do?

Notes

13-4

Day 3
The Amalekites: Our Enemy, Our Battle

Conservative Bible scholars generally agree that the Amalekites represent evil forces opposed to God's people throughout all ages. These forces are categorized as: 1) the flesh; 2) the world; and 3) Satan.

> Read Exodus 17:8-16

THE FLESH

15. What do the following references teach about sin in relation to our flesh? Match the description with the reference (Some may have more than one answer):

    ___ Romans 5:12

    ___ Romans 6:1-7

    ___ Romans 6:11-14

    ___ Romans 8:13

    ___ Galatians 2:20

    ___ Galatians 5:17

    ___ Galatians 5:24-25

    ___ 1 Peter 2:11

    A. Sin is inherited; we are born sinners.

    B. Believers are delivered from sin's power.

    C. Believers still have sinful desires.

    D. Believers must battle against the flesh.

16. Relating these verses to Exodus 17:8-16, what parallels do you see in these truths about our flesh and the Amalekite enemy?

> Read Galatians 5:19-21

17. What are the deeds of the flesh?

    To what specific area in your life is God calling you to do battle against your flesh?

The Lord is my rallying point.

THE WORLD

18. How do these Scripture contribute to your understanding of the term "world"? (See Romans 12:2; Galatians 6:14; Ephesians 2:1-3; 1 John 2:15-17; 5:19.)

19. In what ways are the Amalekites like the world? (Look back to question 8 to compare.)

20. Where in your life are you being too "friendly" with this enemy?

SATAN

21. What does Scripture tell us about our enemy Satan? (Use a topical Bible or concordance.)

22. What parallels do you see in this enemy and the Amalekites in Exodus 17:8-16?

    How are these observations useful in dealing with your enemy Satan?

Deeper Knowledge

Read 1 Samuel 15

List all that the Lord commanded Saul to do.

Record that which Saul neglected and his justification for less than perfect compliance.

What do you think was the real reason for Saul's disobedience?

Taking into consideration the symbolic representation of the Amalekites from today's lesson, along with Saul's response to the command of God, what warnings do you receive for your life?

Puritan John Owen penned, "Kill sin or it be killing you." As recorded in 1 Chronicles 10:13, "Saul died for his trespass which he committed against the LORD." What other Scripture references can you find that support this principle?

How have you seen the truth of this principle confirmed in the lives of others?

In your own life?

Notes

Day 4

Jehovah Nissi Gives the Victory

While God calls the believer to do battle against sin, without Jehovah Nissi fighting for us, victory is impossible.

> Read Exodus 17:14 and Deuteronomy 25:19

23. Fill in the missing words:
    Then the LORD said to Moses, "Write this in a book as a memorial and recite it to Joshua, that _____ will utterly blot out the memory of _____ from under heaven" (Exodus 17:14).

    "Therefore it shall come about when the LORD your God has given you rest from all your surrounding enemies, in the land which the LORD your God gives you as an inheritance to possess, _____ shall blot out the memory of _____ from under heaven; you must not forget" (Deuteronomy 25:19).

24. Identify the similarity and the difference in these two verses.

    How do you explain the seeming contradiction? (See also Deuteronomy 20:3-4; Psalm 44:6-7; Philippians 2:12-13; 1 Timothy 1:18.)

> While God calls the believer to do battle against sin, without Jehovah Nissi fighting for us, victory is impossible.

> Read Exodus 17:8-16 and Numbers 14:40-45

CONTEXT OF THE PASSAGE

In Numbers 14, the Israelites once again encounter the Amalekites in battle. The scene takes place just after the majority of the spies who were sent into the Promised Land returned with a bad report. The Israelites are sentenced to forty years of wandering and dying in the wilderness as the consequence for their sin of unbelief. NOW, they are ready to "obey"!

25. What similarities do you find between Exodus 17:8-16 and Numbers 14:40-45? What differences?

26. What do the following references say about God's role in Isreal's battles?

    Deuteronomy 3:22

    Deuteronomy 20:3-4

    Proverbs 21:31

27. How has your understanding of Jehovah Nissi been enhanced in light of these verses?

    Banner is also defined as standard.

28. From what source(s) do you seek victory in your own battles against sin (flesh, world, Satan)?

    What have been the results—both negative and positive?

    Share a recent victory you found through seeking and relying on Jehovah Nissi.

Day 5
Jesus Is Our Banner

> Read Numbers 21:4-9 and John 3:14-18

29. Describe the scene in Numbers 21:4-9.

30. Explain what Jesus means in John 3:14-15. How is He like the "standard" in Numbers 21?

31. Remembering that Jehovah Nissi means, "The LORD My Banner," explain how Jesus is the ultimate fulfillment of this name of God.

    How is He our "Banner"? (See also John 16:33; Romans 8:37; 1 Corinthians 15:57; 2 Corinthians 2:14.) Include in your answer how Jesus gives us victory.

> "In that day the Root of Jesse will stand as a banner for the peoples; the nations will rally to him, and his place of rest will be glorious."
> Isaiah 11:10, NIV

Read Ephesians 6:10-18

32. List the ways this passage helps you to rally around Christ as your banner.

    Which of these ways will you ask God to help you apply to your life?

Experiencing Knowledge

33. What are some banners that people rally around today?

34. What is your banner? (In what are you putting your trust, seeking fulfillment, and giving credit for your successes?)

35. Identify one area of battle in your life where you will deliberately and actively seek God as your "rallying point." What specifically will you do this week?

36. Write a prayer of confession and commitment to the Lord that He alone will be your Jehovah Nissi.

How does knowledge of this name of God lead you to put you trust in Him (Psalm 9:10)? What specifically will you do today to demonstrate this trust in Jehovah Nissi?

Reflection

Knowing God Through His Names — Lesson Fourteen

JEHOVAH M'KADESH
The Lord Who Sanctifies

Even those who don't usually watch "Antiques Roadshow" can appreciate the drama that unfolded during a stop in Tucson, Arizona. On December 2, 2007, a sweet older gentleman brought in an old blanket for appraisal. Nothing spectacular to look at, it was a plain indigo and white striped primitive blanket that had spent its life draped over a chair. Excitement in his voice, the antiques expert proceeded to explain that this was a "first phase chief's wearing blanket," made between 1840-1860. Worn by a Navajo Chief, this was among the first blankets made of its kind. This old blanket made of common materials sat almost unnoticed in this man's house and was valued upwards of $300,000 - $500,000! Those watching on the edge of their seats could see the genuine shock and tears on the face of this sweet man; he possessed a true treasure, and never dreamed it could have this kind of value.

The value of this blanket was largely due to whom it once belonged. Designed to be worn by a Chief (a person of significance), people place incredible value on it. Just like that blanket, you and I are nothing significant in and of ourselves, but God chose to set us aside for a special purpose. It is the fact that we belong to Him that sets us apart and makes us supremely valuable. So valuable are we in His eyes, that He died on the cross for our behalf.

Do you realize your incredible worth? We are not dependent on some man's opinion to determine our worth or significance in the world. The God who created us took something common and ordinary, and determined that we were worth dying for.

Day 1

Jehovah M'Kadesh, The Lord Who Sanctifies

1. Do you own anything that is precious to you because of to whom it once belonged? What is it and why is it special?

BACKGROUND OF PASSAGE

The introduction to Jehovah M'Kadesh comes on the heels of the Israelites' exodus from Egypt. After a period of four hundred years in slavery under Pharaoh's rule, God miraculously delivered them with Moses' leadership. The Israelites left Egypt, walked through the Red Sea on dry ground, and witnessed God's provision of manna by the time they had encamped at Mount Sinai. Three months after the Exodus (Exodus 19:1), Moses went up to the Mountain of God to receive the Law for the people. After being on the mountain for forty days, God introduces Himself as Jehovah M'Kadesh in His final command to Moses before sending him back to the people.

> Read Exodus 31:12-18

2. What is the command that God gives Moses in these verses?

3. What words or ideas does God associate with the Sabbath? What can you learn from these?

Memory Verse

"'You shall consecrate yourselves therefore and be holy, for I am the LORD your God. You shall keep My statutes and practice them; I am the LORD who sanctifies you.'"

Leviticus 20:7-8

Key Term

Kadesh: The word Kadesh found in the name Jehovah M'Kadesh, translated "sanctify," means to consecrate, sanctify, prepare, dedicate. In this tense it signifies to set apart as sacred, consecrate, dedicate; to observe as holy, keep sacred; to honor as sacred, hallow.

4. Study and summarize what you find about at least one of the words used in the definition of "sanctify" from the sidebar.

Create a sentence about what God has done for you personally as Jehovah M'Kadesh. How does God specifically sanctify you? What impact does this have on your life?

Key Term

Sanctify means to consecrate, prepare and dedicate. In this tense, it signifies to consecrate and dedicate; to observe as holy, keep and honor as sacred.

SABBATH AND SANCTIFICATION

5. What significance do you see in God choosing to introduce this name in a section regarding keeping the Sabbath? How are they connected (Genesis 2:1-3)?

6. How would keeping the Sabbath signify the LORD's sanctifying work?

Deeper Knowledge

Consider the words, "work" and "rest." How do these terms come into play with regard to our salvation and sanctification?

What is the difference between working and resting?

Why does God care that we rest? What principles may He be trying to teach us?

Now go to the New Testament and look for principles regarding "work" and "rest." What insights did you learn?

Day 2
A Light in the Darkness

While Exodus 31:13 is the first time that the name Jehovah M'Kadesh is found in the Bible, some scholars believe Leviticus 20:8 is the most significant. Sometimes called the "Book of Life," the theme of Leviticus centers on the walk of life and worship in relation to God. Adding further importance is the repeated use of Jehovah M'Kadesh; seven out of the ten Old Testament uses are found in Leviticus 20-22.

Read Leviticus 20

This is not a very comfortable chapter to read. It is filled with all kinds of unspeakable wickedness being practiced openly by the people. Yet, God purposely places His name, Jehovah M'Kadesh throughout this section and the two chapters that follow (see 21:8, 15, 23; 22:9, 16, 32).

7. What kinds of sin were being practiced? What command does God repeat in 20:7-8, 23-24 and 26?

8. From what you observed in this passage, what conclusions can you draw as to why God placed Jehovah M'Kadesh there?

9. Thinking about our society, how can we relate to what the Israelites were facing?

10. Just like the Israelites were expected to be set apart from their culture, how can you practically set yourself apart in today's society?

11. Thank God for His active work in setting us apart from the sin around us. Ask Him to use you as a light in a dark world around you.

Notes

Day 3
God's Essential Attribute

The heart of Jehovah M'Kadesh is the truth regarding the holiness of God. "To say the word *holy* twice in Hebrew is to describe someone as 'most holy.' To say the word *holy* three times intensifies the idea to the highest level. In other words, the holiness of God is indescribable in human language. To be *holy* means to be different, distant, or transcendent. Thus the song of the seraphim is a constant refrain that the transcendence of God is indescribable. Although the Lord is totally different from us—He is perfect—in His mercy He still reaches down to take care of us."[1]

God is HOLY. Because He is holy, anything associated with Him must be holy; set apart.

> Read Isaiah 6:1-8

12. What words or phrases does Isaiah use to describe God? How do these point to His holiness?

13. In what ways does Isaiah first respond (verse 5)? What is significant about his response?

14. The word holy means, "different, distant, or transcendent." What are some statements you can make about the connection between a God who is "holy" and Jehovah M'Kadesh, the LORD who sanctifies you?

15. How does this connection impact you?

16. Looking back to the Key Term *sanctify*, what evidences do we see that indicate God was accomplishing this for Isaiah?

17. There is a progression that occurs for Isaiah in this passage. What steps do you see occurring and what is Isaiah's ultimate response (verse 8)?

18. Knowing that God has cleansed us from our sin through the sacrifice of Christ should move us to claim, "Here I am, send me!" What is one way that you have made this claim?

Day 4

Our Spiritual Response

Sanctification follows redemption. There is no sanctification without redemption. There is not genuine redemption that does not result in biblical sanctification. In short, God's will for saints is clear ... to be holy as He is holy. Just like Isaiah, our view of God's holiness should lead to our desire to be holy and serve Him. This involves a delicate balance between what the LORD does and what we do.

19. Record observations from the texts below regarding God's role and the human role in sanctification.

SCRIPTURE	GOD'S ROLE	HUMAN ROLE
Leviticus 20:7-8		
Ezekiel 36:27		
Philippians 2:12-13		

20. Can we take any credit in our own personal sanctification? Why or why not?

Notes

21. Hebrews 12:14 commands us to "pursue ... sanctification." What does it mean to pursue something? What word pictures does this bring up in your mind?

22. What steps do the following verses encourage you to take as you pursue sanctification?

    John 17:17-19

    1 Thessalonians 4:3-4

    2 Timothy 2:21

    1 Peter 1:13-16

> In all ways, Jesus Christ is truly Jehovah M'Kadesh, the LORD who sanctifies us.

23. What is one thing you will do this week to pursue sanctification?

Jesus, Our Jehovah M'Kadesh

It is important to remember that only God produces this kind of change in our lives. It all goes back to Him. We cannot take any of the credit. In all ways, Jesus Christ is truly Jehovah M'Kadesh, the LORD who sanctifies us.

24. Where do you see Jesus as the LORD Who Sanctifies You in the following verses:

    1 Corinthians 6:11

    1 Thessalonians 5:23-24

    Hebrews 10:10-14

25. What are one or two truths from above which really encourage your heart?

HIS POWER IN US

While sanctification is accomplished by God, it does take effort on our part. We must be careful to avoid falling into a life of trying to achieve sanctification by our own efforts. It is God who *has sanctified* us—it is past tense; a done deal. It is only because we are sanctified that we can even respond with a desire for holiness in our daily lives—He gives us that desire and enables us to fulfill it. It is His power that enables you to become more and more holy as He conforms you into the image of His Son. He is Jehovah M'Kadesh.

26. In what ways are you growing in personal holiness? Is there anything you need to let go of in order to continue growing?

Day 5
Set Apart Joy

In our study of Jehovah M'Kadesh, we have looked at God's holiness, His desire for anyone and anything related to Him to be holy, the tension regarding His work and our response in our personal sanctification. Today we will examine what being set apart looks like.

27. Practical sanctification is twofold, a separating *from* something and a separating *to* something else. How do you see this in the following passages?

SCRIPTURE	SEPARATED FROM	SEPARATED TO
John 17:14-19		
2 Corinthians 6:14-7:1		
Colossians 3:5-17		
1 Thessalonians 4:3-7		

"A holy life will make the deepest impression.
Lighthouses blow no horns, they just shine."
Dwight L. Moody

28. Why is it necessary to do both - separate *from* and separate *to*?

29. What are you needing to separate from? How does that look?

30. How do you see your sanctification described in 1 Peter 2:9?

31. What is the ultimate purpose for our sanctification?

You have been set apart for a specific purpose. You have a holy calling. You are no longer a common vessel, but a vessel for honor.

Experiencing Knowledge ⋮ Reflection

32. Like the prophet Isaiah, we should be eager to serve—this is our ultimate joy and pleasure. We have been set apart from the sin of the world to be used by our Savior. Remember, this can be in a variety of settings based on where you are at in your stage of life. Are you being set apart in your home, your marriage, your job, etc.? Why or why not?

33. How does knowledge of this name of God lead you to put your trust in Him (Psalm 9:10)? What specifically will you do today to demonstrate this trust in Jehovah M'Kadesh?

Knowing God Through His Names — Lesson Fifteen

JEHOVAH SHALOM
The Lord Is Peace

A letter appeared in the advice column in a Christian Women's magazine:

Dear Ruth,

I am beginning to question whether God provides for financial needs anymore. We are so far in debt now, that even making minimum payments is proving to be tough.

My husband and I have been married for fifteen years, and we have three wonderful children. We have a fairly good income, and I am able to stay home with the kids. We purchased our current home ten years ago and probably spent more than we should have. It is an effort to make the monthly payments, but our old home *only* had 2,900 square feet, and it was too small for our family. We also had older cars in the past, and we got very tired of them breaking down. With three active kids, I needed transportation I could rely on so we bought nicer ones.

The kids are a bit spoiled. They go to a private school, and many of their friend's families have a lot more money than we do. I just can't bear for them to go without when all of their friends spend money on whatever they want. Also, it seems these days appearance is so much more important than it used to be. However, the only way I can afford to buy clothes is to put them on credit cards.

My husband and I believe in Christ as our Savior, and we attend church regularly. We are starting to argue more about money. We would love to tithe, but that is out of the question in our current situation. So far we have been able to pay our bills, but sometimes only because the credit card companies send checks that I can use for a cash advance.

I can't understand why God would allow us to live in such turmoil. I have been praying that God would provide for our needs, but so far nothing has changed. I am tired of fighting with my husband, and it just tears me up inside to argue with my kids. I would like to talk to our pastor about this, but my husband doesn't want to talk about our finances with anyone. Do you have any advice? Is there anywhere we can turn? **- Troubled Reader**

This "reader" definitely is not experiencing peace in her current situation. Since the creation, mankind has called out to God for His blessing in times of trouble. He desires peace in his circumstances, with no strings attached.

Are peace and a personal relationship with God possible?

Day 1
Israel's Sin

1. Recall and explain a time of noise and confusion in your life when you needed peace and quiet.

BACKGROUND ON THE PASSAGE

In the book of Judges we read of the Israelites' continuing cycle of sinning, repenting and crying out to God for help. Following a forty year period of peace in Israel (Judges 5:31), the Israelites had once again fallen into sin. "The sons of Israel did what was evil in the sight of the LORD" (Judges 6:1). They turned to idolatry, worshiping the gods of the Amorites and corrupting themselves with idolatrous abominations. They had somehow forgotten God's miraculous interventions and guidance in their past. Instead of being devoted to the Lord, they worshiped false gods.

> Read Judges 6:1-6

2. What were the consequences of Israel's sin?

3. How did the sons of Israel attempt to cope within this difficult situation?

4. What was the result of their efforts?

5. How do you think the Israelites were feeling at that moment?

6. What "caves" are you tempted to retreat to in search of peace (someone, something or somewhere)?

Memory Verse

"The LORD will give strength to His people; the LORD will bless His people with peace."

Psalm 29:11

Day 2
Gideon's Call

> Read Judges 6:7-18

7. What reminders were given to the people (verses 8-10)?

8. Why were these important?

9. List the questions Gideon had because God was calling him, and God's responses (verses 13-16).

   GIDEON'S QUESTIONS   GOD'S RESPONSES

   1.

   2.

10. Why did Gideon need a sign that it was God speaking to him? Why was His promise not enough?

11. We all will likely be led by God to perform tasks that are outside our comfort zone. Recall a situation (past or present) where you knew God was asking you to do something you weren't comfortable with.

    What excuses did you make?

    What emotions did you experience?

Key Term

Midian means strife.

15-3

12. In what ways could these verses encourage you when you are called to do something you are uncomfortable with?

    1 Corinthians 1:25-26

    Philippians 4:13

    Hebrews 13:5-6

    1 John 4:4

Day 3

Peace, Perfect Peace

Read Judges 6:19-24

13. What sign was performed?

14. What was God's immediate answer to Gideon's exclamation of fear (verse 23)?

15. What was Gideon's response to God? What name did he call Him?

16. Keeping in mind the definition of Shalom, what happened in Gideon's heart so he could finally experience peace?

"Do you remember the two questions asked by Gideon? If God is for us, why are we so afflicted? Where are all the miracles? The answers to these questions are found in the revelation that Jehovah is peace. The people of Israel had expected that they would experience peace once they had been delivered from Egypt and the wilderness wandering and inhabited the Promised Land. The people of Israel were in the Promised Land but outside the will of God. They had neglected God and ignored His statutes. They were not focused on their unique calling to be about His mission. They didn't understand that peace was not to be found in a physical location, but only in relationship with their creator."[2]

Key Term

Shalom: "The Hebrew word for peace means much more than a cessation of hostilities but carries with it the ideas of well-being, health, and prosperity."[1]

17. Based on your understanding of peace, are you at peace with God? Where is your relationship right now? Take time to write a prayer to Jehovah Shalom.

18. How do you see God fulfill the following roles in these verses?

    Procurer of Peace: Isaiah 53:5

    Personification of Peace: Isaiah 9:6

    Publisher of Peace: Isaiah 52:7

    Perfection of Peace: Isaiah 26:3

    Power of Peace: Isaiah 26:12

    Promise of Peace: Isaiah 32:17

    Perpetuator of Peace: Isaiah 9:7

    (Adapted from an outline by F. E. Marsh)[3]

    Which phrase is most significant to you? Why?

Key Term

Jehovah Shalom: The basic idea underlying the Hebrew word shalom is, "a harmony of relationship or a reconciliation passed upon the completion of a transaction, the payment of a debt, the giving of satisfaction."

It speaks of a spirit of tranquility and freedom from either inward or outward disturbances. God's revelation of Himself as Jehovah Shalom came two hundred years after revealing Himself as Jehovah M'Kaddesh. The people of Israel seemed to have forgotten that they had been set aside for Jehovah's service. Gideon built an altar to the Lord and called it Jehovah Shalom: "Jehovah is, or sends peace." It is implied here that, only in returning to Jehovah, could peace for the individual or the nation be found.[4]

Day 4
Peace Is Possible

Gideon was troubled by his circumstances, yet the LORD gave him peace. Peace, like joy, is not based on circumstances. In the same night Gideon built the altar to Jehovah Shalom, the Lord called on him to begin his task as His warrior. Gideon went forward with the plan knowing it wasn't because of who he was, but because of who God was. We also face times of turmoil, yet God provides for our peace as well.

19. In what type of circumstance are you most likely to lack peace?

20. According to Isaiah 26:3, how is peace possible when you are afraid, worried, distressed or "mired in troubling circumstances"?

Read Philippians 4:6-7

21. The anxiety mentioned means more than concern, but rather a pull in different directions. What is the remedy to these worrisome situations? What is the result if followed?

22. What are you thankful for, and how does that bring peace to a stressful situation?

23. In the following verses, underline what you should do, and circle what God will do for you.

Commit your way to the LORD,
trust also in Him, and He will do it. ~ Psalm 37:5

Cast your burden upon the LORD and He will sustain you;
He will never allow the righteous to be shaken. ~ Psalm 55:22

Commit your works to the LORD
and your plans will be established. ~ Proverbs 16:3

...casting all your anxiety on Him, because He cares for you.
~ 1 Peter 5:7

24. Can you remember a time where you did commit and cast your burden to the Lord? What was the result?

25. Summarize what God would have you do to maintain peace. Commit your situation to the Lord.

Both *commit* and *cast* are from a Hebrew idiom meaning, "roll it over on Jehovah." He can handle it although it's overwhelming for you.

Day 5
Jesus, Our Peace

"Coming to the New Testament we find that Gideon's name for Jehovah, implying that *peace* is not something but *Someone*, not a virtue but a *Person*, is applied to both God and the Lord Jesus."[5]

26. Jesus is the personification of peace. Record what you find in the following verses that reveal the connection between Jesus and peace:

    Isaiah 9:6

    Acts 10:36

    Romans 5:1

    Ephesians 2:13-16

    Colossians 1:19-20

27. Keeping the above references in mind, explain the relationship between Jesus and peace.

28. In what ways does the world try to achieve peace?

29. Read John 14:27 and 16:33. How does Jesus say we can achieve peace?

Deeper Knowledge

Peacemakers

The word *shalom* basically expresses the deepest desire and need of a human life, representing the greatest measure of contentment and satisfaction possible. In its various forms, it appears in Scripture over four hundred times.

We are called to be at peace with one another. What verses can you find on your own that exemplify this calling?

Is there a situation in which you feel called to be a peacemaker?

Experiencing Knowledge

30. Ask the Lord to help you identify areas in your life that are keeping you from experiencing "peace, perfect peace."

31. How does knowledge of this name of God lead you to put your trust in Him (Psalm 9:10)? What will you do today to demonstrate this trust in Jehovah Shalom?

Reflection

Knowing God Through His Names — Lesson Sixteen

JEHOVAH SABAOTH
The Lord of Hosts

"John Paton was a missionary in the New Hebrides Islands. One night hostile natives surrounded the mission station, intent on burning out the Patons and killing them. Paton and his wife prayed during that terror-filled night that God would deliver them. When daylight came they were amazed to see their attackers leave. A year later, the chief of the tribe was converted to Christ. Remembering what had happened, Paton asked the chief what had kept him from burning down the house and killing them. The chief replied in surprise, "Who were all those men with you there?" Paton knew no men were present—but the chief said he was afraid to attack because he had seen hundreds of big men in shining garments with drawn swords circling the mission station."[1]

It was clear to the Indians that night that an army more powerful than their own was willing to fight for the protection of the precious missionaries. By God's choosing, He displayed to the chief and the other warriors that He is Jehovah-Sabaoth. Although we might not see with physical eyes the resources that God uses, He is the One who fights, delivers and rescues. The whole of creation is at His command to accomplish His purposes.

Scripture is clear that believers will face trials and troubles this side of heaven. But, it is also clear that Jehovah-Sabaoth is ready and able to lead us to victory. How encouraging to know that we do not have to fight our battles with our own strength. When we turn to Him for help in the conflicts of life, we can watch expectantly for victory. Our God, Jehovah-Sabaoth, has an infinite abundance of power and might to deliver, rescue and bring victory to His children.

Day 1
Knowing the Lord of Hosts

1. Describe a time when you were faced with a challenge, and someone came to help you succeed.

2. Look up the following verses to discover how the word "host" is used. Pay close attention to what the word is referring to.

Genesis 2:1	
Exodus 7:4	
1 Samuel 17:45	
1 Kings 22:19	
Psalm 103:19-21	
Luke 2:13	

3. What is the significance of God being the commander of these "hosts"?

Read Psalm 89:6-14

4. From this passage, make a list of the descriptive words and phrases used for God.

5. From your list, what insight do you gain about God as Lord of Hosts?

Memory Verse

"Finally, be strong in the Lord and in the strength of His might."

Ephesians 6:10

Key Term

Sabaoth: "The word sabaoth means 'to mass together, to assemble,' the underlying thought being that of warfare. As a general would assemble his army together for combat, so God has His armies, or hosts, that He assembles to fight His cause on earth for the protection of His people. The name Jehovah-Sabaoth is translated, 'The Lord of Hosts,' and it appears more frequently in Scripture than any other of the names of God."[2]

As you begin your study of Jehovah-Sabaoth, remember that warfare is a part of the Christian life. Struggles may arise due to our flesh. Also, this world system and the schemes of the devil seem to constantly attack.

6. How might knowing God as Lord of Hosts encourage you in your battle?

Day 2
A History of Victory

Looking back at Israel's history, there is ample evidence that God was continually providing deliverance and victory. Even though the specific name Lord of Hosts is not found until 1 Samuel, the evidence that He has always been Lord of Hosts is quite obvious.

> Read Joshua 6:1-21

7. What does God declare to Joshua before the siege of Jericho begins (verse 2)?

8. How does Joshua demonstrate that he trusts God to provide the victory?

> Read Judges 7:1-22

9. Why did God keep reducing the number of men in Gideon's army (verse 2)?

10. How do you respond when your own "reserves" are removed?

"Lord of Hosts" is translated "Lord Almighty" in the New International Version and the New Living Translations of the Bible.

11. What was the result of Gideon's obedience to God's plan (verses 19-22)?

12. How can both the victories experienced by Joshua and Gideon be credited only to God?

13. Where can you clearly identify a victory in your life that God alone produced?

14. How has experiencing God's victory in your struggles affected your faith?

Day 3
Getting to Know the Lord of Hosts

God is first specifically referred to as Lord of Hosts in 1 Samuel 1. At this time, Israel was spiritually floundering. The priesthood that God had instituted was corrupt and the role of the judges had been compromised by dishonesty. The people's failure to put their trust in God's plan led them to look for victory and prosperity elsewhere. As often is the case, even in the midst of spiritual darkness there was a faithful few who continued to trust. At this time of national rebellion, we find a godly woman in the midst of her own intimate, personal struggle. Her cry to the Lord of Hosts reveals that she understood that God cared about the internal battle she was facing. She trusted Him to bring victory and deliverance.

Hannah trusted the Lord of Hosts...

> Read 1 Samuel 1:1-19

15. What difficulties was Hannah experiencing? (List some emotions as well.)

16. What evidence shows that Hannah understood that God was in control of her circumstances? Why is that important?

Notes

17. What does Hannah do to deal with her difficult situation (verse 15)?

18. What do you do to address difficult situations in your life?

19. Describe Hannah's behaviors and attitudes in verses 18-19.

20. What ended up changing her feelings?

If you continue reading in 1 Samuel, you will see that God did give Hannah the son she prayed for. As she vowed, Hannah also gave up her son, Samuel, to the service of the Lord for "all the days of his life" (1 Samuel 1:11). It seems that Hannah's victory in this difficult struggle was not founded only in the answered prayer for a child, but also her attitude was transformed as a result of worshipping God as Lord of Hosts, the Deliverer (1 Samuel 1:15-18).

21. Recall a time when God gave you a victorious attitude in the midst of struggle. How did this change affect your outlook of the situation?

Day 4

David Exalts the Lord of Hosts

After God's favor was removed from King Saul, another was anointed to become the future king of Israel. This future king was a shepherd boy named David.

> Read 1 Samuel 17:1-25

22. Describe the challenge put before Israel's army. What caused the greatest concern?

23. How did Saul and his army react? How should have Saul reacted?

24. What were the people focusing on?

25. What do you tend to focus on when faced with a challenging situation?

> Read 1 Samuel 17:31-50

26. How had David previously experienced God's deliverance in his role as shepherd?

27. What actions revealed that David was trusting in God's power to defeat his enemy?

Notes

28. Why was David so confident of the outcome of the battle?

29. Reflect on Saul's response and David's response in this situation. As you face "giants" in your life, what do your attitudes and actions reveal about your belief in God as Lord of Hosts?

30. What would God have you continue to do to cultivate an increasingly confident faith in God as Lord of Hosts?

Day 5
Victory Today

31. Review the Old Testament characters discussed in this lesson. Fill in the chart to compare and contrast their circumstances and interactions with the Lord of Hosts.

"BATTLE" SUMMARY	EVIDENCE OF GOD'S VICTORY	THEIR RESPONSE
Joshua		
Gideon		
Hannah		
David		

Notes

32. Which person, or circumstance were you most able to relate to? In what ways?

33. How has God used these illustrations this week to increase your trust in Him?

JESUS, THE LORD OF HOSTS

"Did we in our own strength confide, Our striving would be losing, Were not the right man on our side, The man of God's own choosing. Dost ask who that may be? Christ Jesus, it is He - Lord Sabaoth His name, From age to age the same, And He must win the battle."[3]

This precious hymn reflects truth found in the Scriptures that believers experience victory in this life because of Christ's work on the cross. Because of His victory over sin and death, we can walk in victory daily, and look forward to resting in victory when our battles are over and we are enjoying eternity with our Lord and Savior.

34. How has Christ revealed Himself as Lord of Hosts in your life?

> "Did we in our own strength confide,
> Our striving would be losing,
> Were not the right man on our side,
> The man of God's own choosing.
> Dost ask who that may be?
> Christ Jesus, it is He
> Lord Sabaoth His name,
> From age to age the same,
> And He must win the battle."[4]

Deeper Knowledge

Use Scripture and a commentary, dictionary or other Bible resource to expand your understanding of the armor of God as listed in Ephesians 6:13-17. Here are some ideas for areas of further study: the significance of each piece as used in physical battles, the spiritual importance of individual pieces, and practical ways that believers "put on" and "take up" this armor.

Experiencing Knowledge

35. What is the most encouraging truth you have learned about the Lord of Hosts? How can this strengthen you in the battles to come?

36. How does knowledge of this name of God lead you to put your trust in Him (Psalm 9:10)? What specifically will you do today to demonstrate this trust in Jehovah Sabaoth?

Reflection

Knowing God Through His Names

JEHOVAH RAAH
The Lord My Shepherd

The cold weather provided a great opportunity for the Howard family to go spelunking. Off they went to the Oregon Caves to explore and escape the cold. As they descended deeper into the cave, the darker it became. Before they knew it, complete darkness enveloped them. Not able to see the hand in front of her, seven-year-old Sarah became frightened. Trying to be brave, she suppressed her desire to cry out for help. She knew the walls of the cave were closing in. Why did her brother insist on turning off the flashlights anyway? Her heart started pounding, and the pupils of her eyes were getting larger by the second, trying to take in any shred of light, but there was none to be had.

Sarah felt like she was all alone. Frightened, she started to call for help. Before the words could escape her shivering lips, she felt her father's hand grab hers. What comfort it brought her knowing that her dad was there to guide her, to protect her. She recognized his touch, surely she was safe. It no longer mattered that she couldn't see what lay ahead, her father was there. He would provide all that she needed. She had no doubt.

The same is true for believers; no matter where we are or what our needs, Jehovah Raah, "the Lord our Shepherd" is there to guide us, provide for us, and walk with us.

Day 1
Meeting the Shepherd

1. When have you benefited from a tour guide?

BACKGROUND OF THE PASSAGE

Psalm 23, perhaps one of the most well-known Psalms, portrays the name of Jehovah in the most intimate of ways. Jehovah Raah, The Lord My Shepherd, is described by David.

"It is a psalm of David. It could not have come as appropriately out of the experience of anyone else in the Old Testament. Perhaps it was written in the latter years of Israel's great Shepherd King, the forerunner and type of that Great Shepherd of the sheep, David's greater Son. It has the ring of a full experience, of a faith sobered by trials, and a life mellowed by the passing years. He looks back upon the stormy, troubled years when his life was hunted by the inveterate enemy Saul; then through the years of warfare and rebellion, of sordid sin and sorrow; and finds God's goodness and guiding presence through it all. Then recalling the occupation of his own childhood and youth, that of caring for his father's sheep, he can find no more beautiful and fitting analogy of Jehovah's relationship to himself than that of a shepherd to the sheep. And now after the storm and stress of years through which Jehovah has so safely and successfully brought him, with confident faith he can look forward to the years ahead and say: 'Surely goodness and mercy shall follow me all the days of my life.'"[1]

> Read Psalm 23

2. List the qualities of a shepherd that are revealed in this psalm.

3. Record the different aspects of a shepherd's role.

Psalm 78:52-53	
Isaiah 40:11	
Ezekiel 34:11-12	
Ezekiel 34:14-15	

Memory Verse

"So we Your people and the sheep of Your pasture will give thanks to You forever; to all generations we will tell of Your praise."

Psalm 79:13

Key Term

Jehovah-Raah means, "Lord my Shepherd." The principle meaning of "raah" is to feed or lead to pasture. It first appears in a very personal way in Psalm 23.

4. **Why is it important for the shepherd to be capable of fulfilling his role?**

5. **In what areas are you able to identify that God is at work in your life as a shepherd?**

It is assumed that if God is the shepherd, then we are sheep. There are many references in Scripture that compare human beings with sheep.

6. **According to Psalm 119:176; Isaiah 53:6 and 1 Peter 2:25, why do we need a shepherd?**

   How is this true in your life?

> It is assumed that if God is the shepherd, then we are sheep. There are many references in Scripture that compare human beings with sheep.

Day 2
The Shepherd Guides His Sheep

Read Psalm 23 again today. Pay close attention to verses 2 and 3.

"He makes me lie down in green pastures; He leads me beside quiet waters. He restores my soul; He guides me in the paths of righteousness for His name's sake."

THE SHEPHERD GUIDES HIS SHEEP ... BY HIS WORD

7. **Consider Psalm 19:7-11. This short section of Scripture reveals a wealth of truth concerning the guidance and nourishment that is found in God's Word.**

	SYNONYMS FOR GOD'S WORD	DESCRIPTION OF GOD'S WORD	BENEFIT TO OUR LIFE
Psalm 19:7			
Psalm 19:8			
Psalm 19:9			

17-3

8. In the past six months, how have you experienced the benefits of allowing the Word of God to guide and lead you?

THE SHEPHERD GUIDES HIS SHEEP ... BY HIS SPIRIT

Read Ephesians 1:13

9. When was the Holy Spirit given to you?

Read John 14:16

10. How is the Holy Spirit described? What does this suggest about our condition as "sheep"?

11. How long is the Spirit's help available to believers?

12. In what ways do these truths encourage you to allow the Spirit to guide?

13. Fill in the blanks to complete John 16:13: "But when He, the Spirit of _____, comes, He will guide you into all the _____; for He will not speak on His own initiative, but whatever He hears, He will speak; and He will disclose to you what is to come."

Notes

14. What assurance does this give you concerning the direction of the Spirit's guidance in your life?

15. How can you make yourself more available to the Shepherd's guidance through His Word and Spirit?

Day 3
The Shepherd Protects His Sheep

As you read Psalm 23 today, focus your attention on verse 4.

"Even though I walk through the valley of the shadow of death, I fear no evil, for You are with me; Your rod and Your staff, they comfort me."

THE SHEPHERD PROTECTS HIS SHEEP ... BY HIS PRESENCE

16. Just as a shepherd is with his sheep, you can be confident that Jehovah Raah is with you. As you read the following verses, fill in the chart below telling how His presence is described.

Psalm 32:7	
Psalm 46:1	
Psalm 91:1	
Psalm 145:18	

17. Which of these descriptions encourages you in your current circumstances?

18. How has the Shepherd's presence been a source of protection in your life?

> "Even though I walk through the valley of the shadow of death, I fear no evil, for You are with me; Your rod and Your staff, they comfort me."

THE SHEPHERD PROTECTS HIS SHEEP ... BY DISCIPLINING

The shepherd used his rod and staff to correct and redirect the sheep when they strayed. The rod and staff served as tools for discipline in the Shepherd's hand. In much the same way, God disciplines His children for their good.

"You can trust the Shepherd to be concerned only for your care and protection. We often forget that God's discipline is always prompted by His unchanging love and is always consistent with His character. He must lead us back onto the right paths so that we will know His presence and experience His protection."[2]

19. Study Hebrews 12:3-11. Using these verses, develop a definition for the term discipline.

20. How is biblical discipline a form of protection?

21. Review Hebrews 12:10b-11. What can we look forward to if we endure and submit to the Lord's discipline process?

Deeper Knowledge

Use a commentary, Bible encyclopedia, or other resource to research the significance of *tablelands* in relation to a shepherd and his sheep. Apply what you learn to make a list of what the Shepherd's *table* provides today (i.e. grace, mercy). Use Scripture to support your answers.

Day 4

Intimacy with the Good and Loving Shepherd

As an honored guest at the table of His shepherd, David concludes the Shepherd's psalm with a picture of an intimate relationship between him and his shepherd; a relationship that would continue all the days of his life.

Review Psalm 23, and concentrate on verses 5 and 6.

"You prepare a table before me in the presence of my enemies; You have anointed my head with oil; my cup overflows. Surely goodness and lovingkindness will follow me all the days of my life, and I will dwell in the house of the LORD forever."

23. **The word "surely" in the Hebrew text means "only." Cross out the word "surely" and replace it with the word "only." Now reread the verse aloud. As you understand that "only" goodness and lovingkindness will follow you, how does this impact your life?**

24. **Refer to the sidebar. How does the definition of "will follow" help you understand the Shepherd's pursuit of His sheep? In addition, read Colossians 1:13. What does this verse show in regard to His pursuit of us?**

25. **Read Psalm 145. Make a list of how the Shepherd shows His goodness and lovingkindness.**

26. **Pick three characteristics from the list above. When has God displayed His goodness and lovingkindness to you in those particular ways?**

In the Hebrew text, the definition of the phrase "will follow" means to "pursue ardently; aim eagerly to secure; pursue." Webster's Dictionary defines ardent as "intensely enthusiastic or devoted; zealous."

27. How does remembering and reflecting on the goodness of the Shepherd affect your response to a particular circumstance you are facing today?

Day 5
Jesus, Our Good Shepherd

In Psalm 23, David describes Jehovah Raah - The Lord our Shepherd, from a sheep's point of view. Jesus describes Himself as the fulfillment of the Shepherd in John 10.

Read John 10:1-17

28. Record the characteristics of the care of the following individuals. Also, record the results of their care.

	THE TYPE OF CARE GIVEN	THE RESULT
Thieves and Robbers		
Strangers		
The Hired Hands		
Jesus		

29. What is the major difference between the care of Jesus and the others?

Notes

30. Reflecting on the chart, in what ways have you experienced the care of the Good Shepherd in your life? Thank Him for His shepherding in your life.

31. How should a genuine sheep respond to the Good Shepherd (John 10:3-4, 14)?

    How are you living daily by these simple truths?

Experiencing Knowledge

32. Praise God for Jesus, who is both the Lamb of God and the Good Shepherd, and for all the benefits that are yours as a result.

33. How does knowledge of this name of God lead you to put your trust in Him (Psalm 9:10)? What specifically will you do today to demonstrate this trust in Jehovah Raah?

Reflection

Knowing God Through His Names

The door opened just a crack. Peeking out from behind it, Samantha could see two dark nervous eyes. The petite lady opened the door a bit wider. Appearing much older than her age, it was obvious life had dealt its blows. Samantha was knocking at her door because the woman had called the church asking for help.

Sam gathered from their conversation that the woman was relatively new to town. She had no friends, and no longer had any relationship with the son or daughter she had left behind. Life to her was empty, cruel, and held no hope. Sam found herself wondering about the events of this lady's life, and the regrets she now carried with her.

Just the week before, Sam had walked into the hospital room of another woman, Virginia. Although Virginia was suffering from the results of several mini-strokes, her eyes twinkled and her smile lit up the hospital room. She spoke of Jesus and His care for her. Sam joined in as Virginia sang hymns of praise to her Father. Virginia had been thankful for her life and the many ways God had provided for her.

Sam couldn't help but notice the contrast between these two women. Each one surrounded by their own difficult circumstances; one hopeless and hardened, and one with such joy and peace. Only Jesus could make that kind of difference.

The people of Judah found themselves in much the same place as the woman with the dark, nervous eyes. They had lived lives full of regret that left them hopeless. Yet God made a promise to them, that He would be Jehovah Tsidkenu, "The Lord Our Righteousness." What hope that brought. What a difference the fulfillment of that promise makes in our lives today.

Day 1
There Is None Righteous

1. When have you received something you absolutely did not deserve?

BACKGROUND OF THE PASSAGE

The northern tribes of Israel had been taken into captivity a hundred years prior. Now Judah was about to face the same predicament. All of Judah, except a small remnant, was in a state of spiritual and moral decay. The people refused to obey God's Word, and they had lost all interest in spiritual things.

God sent Jeremiah as His spokesperson to the people of Judah. Jeremiah proclaimed the news that God would use Babylon to bring judgment on Judah by allowing the Babylonians into the city to attack. Those that survived would face severe consequences for the sin and rebellion of the entire nation.

Read Jeremiah 21:1-10

2. What consequences were the people of Judah about to face?

Read Jeremiah 32:16-35

3. List the character traits of God that are revealed in verses 17-22.

4. How did the people of Judah respond to the Lord (verses 23, 33-35)?

Memory Verse

"He made Him who knew no sin to be sin on our behalf, so that we might become the righteousness of God in Him."

2 Corinthians 5:21

5. What were the consequences going to be for their disobedience (verses 24-35)?

6. The attitude and actions of the Judeans are much like people today. In the text below, circle the word that is repeated most often.

   "What then? Are we better than they? Not at all; for we have already charged that both Jews and Greeks are all under sin; as it is written, 'THERE IS NONE RIGHTEOUS, NOT EVEN ONE; THERE IS NONE WHO UNDERSTANDS, THERE IS NONE WHO SEEKS FOR GOD; ALL HAVE TURNED ASIDE, TOGETHER THEY HAVE BECOME USELESS; THERE IS NONE WHO DOES GOOD, THERE IS NOT EVEN ONE.'" Romans 3:9-12

   What conclusion can you draw about yourself based on these verses?

7. In what ways are you similar to the men and women of Judah?

8. According to Romans 6:23, what are the consequences for your disobedience and sin?

9. If this was the end of the story for the people of Judah and for you, what emotions might you experience? What kind of hope would you have?

   Read Romans 6:23 again. What is our hope?

Key Term

Righteousness: "'The character or quality of being right or just.' It was formerly spelled, 'rightwiseness,' which clearly expresses the meaning. It is used to denote an attribute of God, e.g., Romans 3:5, the context of which shows that, 'the righteousness of God' means essentially the same as His faithfulness or truthfulness, which is consistent with His own nature and promises. Romans 3:25-26 speaks of His 'righteousness' as exhibited in the Death of Christ. This is sufficient to show men that God is neither indifferent to sin nor regards it lightly. On the contrary, it demonstrates that quality of holiness in Him which must find expression in His condemnation of sin."[1]

Day 2

God's Promise and Provision of Righteousness

The Psalmist declared in Psalm 30:5, "His anger is but for a moment, His favor is for a lifetime." Surely the people of Judah experienced God's anger. For seventy years they lived in exile (Jeremiah 29:10). Yet God's favor returned.

Read Jeremiah 32:36-33:13

10. List what God promises to provide for the men and women of Judah.

11. What do these provisions reveal about God and His desire for His people?

Read Jeremiah 33:14-16

12. How did God intend to fulfill His promise?

Deeper Knowledge

There are other places in Scripture that speak of the "Branch." Look up Isaiah 4:2; Jeremiah 23:5-6; and Zechariah 3:8. What further insight do you gain about the Branch of David?

Notes

13. What name does God use to reveal Himself?

14. What does God's name indicate about how He will keep His promise to His people?

JESUS, OUR RIGHTEOUSNESS

15. What insight does Galatians 4:4-5 give about how the Lord is our righteousness?

16. 2 Corinthians 5:21 speaks of the "great exchange" that took place when God fulfilled His promise to be the Lord our Righteousness. Read 2 Corinthians 5:21 and in your own words describe what was exchanged. Why was that necessary and what was the result? Use additional Scripture to support your statement.

17. Write out a prayer of thanksgiving to the Lord.

The Great Exchange
Isaiah 53

- He was wounded so I might be healed.
- He was rejected so I could be accepted.
- He carried my sorrows so I could be comforted.
- He was punished so I might have peace.
- He took my sins so I could be declared righteous.

Day 3

Pursue Righteous Living

> Read 1 Peter 2:24

18. What two characteristics should be present in the life of someone who has trusted Christ to be their righteousness?

DIE TO SIN

Living a new life of righteousness requires dying to sin.

> Read Romans 6:1-14

19. What specific truths does Paul say a believer must know (verses 3-11)?

20. In what ways does this knowledge encourage you to die to sin?

RIGHTEOUS LIVING

Dying to sin provides the opportunity to live righteously; a life that is in a right relationship with God.

21. Make a list of sinful activities and attitudes someone would run from if they were seeking righteous living.

> Read 1 Timothy 6:6-12

22. Prayerfully review your list above. Ask God to show you how any of these are keeping you from living the righteous life Jesus provided. Confess, and ask God to replace that sin with a desire to live righteously.

Notes

23. What would God desire you pursue instead (verses 11-12)?

Pursuing righteous living goes much deeper than following rules; at the heart is a relationship with the One who *is* our righteousness.

> Read Philippians 3:7-11

24. What is the one thing that motivated Paul? Do you have the same motivation? On a scale of 1 to 10, to what degree do you share this pursuit? (1 being not at all and 10 being completely)

25. According to Matthew 5:6, what kind of a longing should you have toward righteous living? What do the descriptive words reveal about a believer's desire?

26. Consider your own need to live righteously. What motivates you? What keeps you from pursuing righteousness? Write a prayer asking God to increase your desire and relationship with the One who is your righteousness.

> Pursuing righteous living goes much deeper than following rules; at the heart is a relationship with the One who *is* our righteousness.

Day 4
Benefits of Righteous Living

> Read Titus 3:3-7

27. List the characteristics of someone's life before knowing Christ as their Savior.

28. Describe what the state of your life would be apart from Christ.

29. What did God do to intervene (verses 4-7)?

30. What did you have to do with God's intervention in your own life (verse 5)?

Living a life of righteousness would never be possible apart from God's provision. It is more than an obligation or drudgery. Living righteously is a special privilege provided by God for all who have believed in Jesus as their Savior.

31. In the chart below, record the blessings that God provides for living righteously.

VERSE	BLESSING
2 Chronicles 16:9	
Psalm 92:12	
Proverbs 10:24-25	
Proverbs 14:32	
Proverbs 18:10	
James 5:16	
1 Peter 3:12	

32. Because of what Christ did, believers can live righteously. Based on the previous verses, write a description of the life of one who pursues righteous living.

Notes

33. Compare your answers to question #29 with question #33. Take a moment to thank the Lord for the difference He has made, and can make, in your life.

Day 5
Praising God for His Righteousness

34. Investigate a Bible character that believes in God as their Jehovah Tsidkenu. In what ways were their lives changed? List characteristics of their life before they believed in God and the characteristics after they believed in God.

Read Colossians 1:13-14

35. Rewrite this passage by replacing the words "us" and "we" and "we" with "me" and "I".

36. What has God accomplished on *your* behalf?

37. In what ways is your life different as a result of knowing Jehovah Tsidkenu?

> "For He rescued us from the domain of darkness, and transferred us to the kingdom of His beloved Son, in whom we have redemption, the forgiveness of sins."
> Colossians 1:13-14

Experiencing Knowledge

39. What steps will you take to allow God's many accomplishments to impact your life to a greater degree?

40. How does knowledge of this name of God lead you to put your trust in Him (Psalm 9:10)? What will you do today to demonstrate this trust in Jehovah Tsidkenu?

Reflection

Knowing God Through His Names  Lesson Nineteen

JEHOVAH SHAMMAH
The Lord Is There

The day of November 14th will forever be emblazoned in Christy's mind. That morning her husband told her he was feeling "funny," and as the day progressed, the headache he'd been experiencing continued to worsen. Both nurses, they talked about the possibilities of what it might be, but decided they'd wait to see if the symptoms got worse. By evening, Tom was laying on the floor whimpering, holding his head because of the pain. When Christy returned from taking her son to a soccer pizza party and saw Tom, she made a quick decision to take him to the hospital. Never had she seen him in such pain. It tore at her heart to see her beloved of 20 years hurting. As she helped Tom up, he could barely walk. His balance was completely gone and he felt nauseated. As they drove to the hospital, Christy prayed to God and asked for help! "Lord, I don't know what is happening, but I know You do, and that You are Tom's ultimate healer. Help me to remember that You aren't surprised, and that You are with us as we go through this."

After a couple hours of testing at the hospital, Tom was diagnosed as having survived a stroke. The clot had formed because of a known heart defect and had found its way into his brain. The doctors told Christy that it was a very small clot and it looked like the only function adversely affected was his balance. It could have been so much worse.

A week later, Christy was sitting at her desk looking out the window and going over the events of the previous week. It stood out in her mind how God had been with them every step of the way. The doctor on call had been Tom and Christy's doctor for the last 15 years and knew Tom's health history. The clot was small and had affected an area that would soon heal. Family and friends had surrounded them with such love, prayer, and help over the last week. Christy found herself tearing up just thinking about all the ways God had met their needs. She worshipped Him right then and there, thanking Him for His presence during that time, and for pouring out such heavenly love through ordinary people. She knew that she couldn't have gone through that difficult time with such peace if it hadn't been for God's presence.

Ezekiel 48 tells us how in the MilleniumJerusalem which will be a large city with our Lord as the center. He will reign from His throne (Jeremiah 3:17). There will be no tears, no pain, no sickness, no curse, no sin. We will be at rest in His presence. What reasons to rejoice! In the meantime, our amazing God has provided us individually with His presence, the Holy Spirit. Jehovah Shammah, "The Lord is There."

Day 1

God's Presence - Our Need and His Desire

1. **Describe a time when you could have been lonely, but the presence of a friend made a difference.**

As believers, we look forward to the day when Christ will one day reign over all the nations. Jehovah Shammah! The Lord is there! He will one day reign over ALL the earth. We will see Him as He really is. We will see His glory! This is God's desire, after all. He desires us to be with Him for all eternity. This is what motivated the cross. God provided so that we would NEVER be separated from Him again.

Throughout history, God has been present with the people who love and follow Him. We see God walking with Adam and Eve, Moses and the Israelites, Jesus present on earth, the Holy Spirit living in those who believe, and then Christ's reign in the New Jerusalem. What a magnificent testimony to the uniqueness of our God. God desires us, as His creation, to be with Him. He desires for us to see His glory, and to share in the amazing love the Father and Son have for us. As believers, we place our hope in the knowledge that one day we will be ushered into God's holy presence.

BACKGROUND

God declared to Moses, "I have surely seen the affliction of My people who are in Egypt, and have given heed to their cry because of their taskmasters, for I am aware of their sufferings. So I have come down to deliver them from the power of the Egyptians, and to bring them up from that land to a good and spacious land, to a land flowing with milk and honey" (Exodus 3:7-8a).

So begins the epic journey of Moses and the Children of Israel, and God's presence among a people of His choosing. Moses and the Israelites would witness God's powerful presence, provision, pardon, and justice on earth, while on the road to the land of promise, which God had set aside for His people.

2. **In the chart on the next page, record the form of God's presence and the impact God's presence had on the people.**

Memory Verse

"But as for me, the nearness of God is my good; I have made the Lord GOD my refuge, that I may tell of all Your works."

Psalm 73:28

REFERENCE	FORM OF GOD'S PRESENCE	IMPACT ON THE PEOPLE
Exodus 3:1-9		
Exodus 13:17-22		
Exodus 19:1-25		

3. Summarize what God's presence provided for His people.

4. What did God require of those that came into His presence (Exodus 19:10-15)?

5. Note the impact God's presence had on His people. What impact does God's presence in your life have on you?

    How do you feel you are set apart from those around you who aren't seeking Him? Consider what your life would be apart from God.

Although God had shown His presence in a powerful way on Mt. Sinai (Exodus 19) when He gave His commandments to Moses, the Israelites became restless and built a golden calf, a "god," to lead them into the Promised Land. God's wrath burned against them for their lack of faith. Moses entreated God to turn from His anger and reminded God of His promise to Abraham. God graciously listened and turned from His anger. Yet God's people continued to sin.

Read Exodus 33:1-6

6. What did God declare to Moses concerning His presence and help in the future?

"I will dwell in them and *walk* among them; and I will be their God and they shall be My people."
2 Corinthians 6:16

7. Although God has promised believers that He would never leave them or forsake them (Hebrews 13:5), what effect does sin have on a believer's relationship with God (1 John 1:5-8)?

   What is the remedy for restoring that relationship (1 John 1:9)?

   Examine your own heart. Is there anything hindering your relationship with the Lord? Confess it, and turn from it.

Day 2
God's Presence in the Past - Meeting the Needs of His People

Previously appearing as a cloud and pillar of fire, God planned and provided for a more regal residence for Himself during the journey to the Promised Land (Exodus 25-31:11; 35:4-40:35). In Exodus 40:34-38, God's presence comes to rest on the tabernacle, and then later in 2 Chronicles, God comes and dwells in an even more permanent building - the temple that Solomon built. God dwelt among the people until the decline of Israel. As a result of sin, the Israelites were taken into captivity and the temple, which represented God's presence with them, was destroyed. The years spent in Babylonian captivity left the Israelites physically, emotionally, and spiritually bankrupt. In the absence of God Himself, God sent Ezekiel to declare the Word of the Lord at a time when the nation of Israel was decimated.

Read Ezekiel 22:1-14

8. List the sins the Israelites committed.

9. What could the Israelites anticipate as a result of their sins (Ezekiel 24:14)?

Notes

10. God still desired restoration and a relationship with the Israelites. What instructions did God give them in Ezekiel 33:11?

11. God graciously promises restoration to His people upon their repentance (Ezekiel 36:8-10). What promises does God make to the Israelites in Ezekiel 36:24-27?

12. Chapters 40-48 in Ezekiel reveal God's plan for restoration, focusing on a detailed description of a new temple that symbolizes God's presence among them, concluding with a revelation of a new name for God (Ezekiel 48:35). Jehovah Shammah, meaning, "The Lord is There," is revealed for the first time. What message would this name bring to the exiled Israelites?

13. How does knowing God as Jehovah Shammah encourage you today?

"And the Word became flesh, and dwelt among us, and we saw His glory, glory as of the only begotten from the Father, full of grace and truth."

John 1:14

Day 3
God's Presence in the Flesh, Jesus!

Throughout the Old Testament God revealed Himself to His people in various ways: through a cloud, a burning bush, and in the promise of His name, Jehovah Shammah, "The Lord is There." In the Gospels we see God in the flesh, in the form of His Son, Jesus, who walked and talked and lived with people. Jesus is Jehovah Shammah. In John 4 and 5 we see Jesus stopping to talk with two very lonely people. Struggling in their sin and infirmities all on their own, Jesus stopped and took time to talk to them and meet their needs. For a moment in time they were in the presence of the God of the universe, the One who came to seek and save the lost, and they left His presence, changed forever.

> Read John 4:1-42

14. What indicators do you find in this passage that the woman at the well was very much alone in life?

15. What do we learn about this woman from her conversation with Jesus?

16. In what ways did Jesus show love and care for this woman?

17. As you have spent time in God's presence the last few weeks, how has He shown His love and care for you?

> Read John 5:1-15

18. What did the man by the pool have in common with the woman at the well?

19. How was the interaction between Jesus and this man different from the interaction between Jesus and the woman at the well?

    What do these differences indicate about how God responds to the individual needs of people?

20. Just as the presence of Jesus changed these two people, how does spending time in God's presence change you?

Take a few moments to thank the Lord for His presence in your life, and the impact He has had in your life.

Notes

Day 4

God's Presence in the Present

God's presence was seen in spectacular forms throughout the Old Testament. Jesus walked on earth in the New Testament, yet the time had come for Him to depart. His disciples were tempted to despair. What would they do without Jesus by their side?

> Read John 14:16-20

21. What promise did Jesus make to His disciples to encourage them about His departure?

22. In what ways would Jesus' departure actually be of benefit to the disciples and to all believers (see also John 16:7)?

23. In the chart below, record the purpose of the Holy Spirit in your life.

SCRIPTURE	PURPOSE OF THE HOLY SPIRIT IN MY LIFE
John 16:13-14	
Romans 8:5-6	
2 Corinthians 1:22	
Galatians 5:16-17	
Galatians 5:22-25	
1 John 4:12-16	

The indwelling Holy Spirit enables believers to reveal Jesus to those around them. God has provided His Spirit so that Jehovah Shammah would be seen in us every day!

Notes

> ## Deeper Knowledge
>
> **Read Isaiah 11:1-3**
> Find and list six characteristics of the Holy Spirit in this passage. Using a concordance, do a word study on each attribute.
>
> Spend some time meditating on these Scriptures, thanking Jehovah Shammah for the ways that His presence helps you.

Day 5

God's Presence in the Future – Maranatha!

Read John 14:1-3

24. What encouragement and hope for the future did Jesus provide for the disciples and us?

Meanwhile, we wait and long for that day, along with all creation.

THE LONGING OF ALL CREATION

25. In the chart below, record who/what is longing, and what they are longing for.

	WHO/WHAT IS LONGING	WHAT ARE THEY LONGING FOR?
Romans 8:18-25		
Philippians 1:21-24		
2 Corinthians 5:1-2		

Evaluate your own longings and desires. While you wait for the ultimate fulfillment of Jehovah Shammah, what are you longing for?

How do your longings compare with those recorded above?

Notes

26. Based on Revelation 21:1-5, 10-11, 22-23 and 22:1-5, write a description in your own words of the heavenly city, Jerusalem, and what your life will be like when you are there in the presence of the Lord.

27. God's presence is certainly something to look forward to! What a celebration that will be! In the meantime, God has provided His Spirit and given us instructions on what we are to be doing while we wait for that day when we will see Jesus face to face. According to 1 John 2:28-29 and 4:15-17, what does John command us to do while we wait for that time we'll be in God's presence for all eternity?

What steps will you take this week to "wait" according to these instructions?

Experiencing Knowledge

28. Take a few moments to reflect. In what ways does your lifestyle demonstrate that God is present in you? Consider your relationships, business activities, leisure activities, the words that you use, priorities, etc.

29. How does the knowledge of this name of God lead you to put your trust in Him (Psalm 9:10)? What specifically will you do today to demonstrate this trust in Jehovah Shammah?

> God's presence is certainly something to look forward to! What a celebration that will be! In the meantime, God has provided His Spirit and given us instructions on what we are to be doing while we wait for that day when we will see Jesus face to face.

Knowing God Through His Names

Lesson Twenty

PATER
Father

Cleo never really knew her father. All she remembered was that he had a rather warm smile and she thought he liked to sing. "*But, was that true?*" she wondered. Or, was that what she imagined about the man in the picture she still carried? Was he the same man that left her mother and two older siblings when she was only three? She was *sure* he *must* have loved her. "*But, why was it again that he left? Mom said that liquor and gambling were very important to him. But how could that be?*" She was sure that he had been kind to her. "*How sad that he suffered that heart attack and died so young.*" This distant figure in her childhood memory was her father, *but* . . . he was a stranger.

Cleo knew that her best friend, Marni, had a very different father. Marni often spoke about him and sometimes related thoughts about her dad to thoughts she had about God. Her father had been quite a harsh disciplinarian, and yet, Marni seemed to harbor nothing but adoration for her dad. She had shared with Cleo how the same strong arms that pulled her around for a spanking had also held her tight and carried her when she was weary or hurt. Marni was fully confident that her dad would have given his life for her had circumstances ever called for it.

These two friends both had faith in Jesus Christ, His death, burial and resurrection. They both understood themselves to be sinners and they shared in the joy of knowing Christ as Savior. But, Cleo longed to know God as her Heavenly Father; she wondered if she ever could.

Even though Cleo had a difficult time relating to her earthly father, God reveals Himself in the New Testament as our **Pater** — a Father who desires a relationship with us.

Day 1
Personal Father

1. What characteristics have you seen in your earthly father (or another father figure) that have had an influence on your perception of our Heavenly Father?

2. Looking at the relationship of the Father to His people in the Old Testament, fill in the chart below. Identify who His relationship is with and what role He has.

SCRIPTURE REFERENCE	ROLE OF THE FATHER
Deuteronomy 32:6	
Isaiah 63:16	
Isaiah 64:8	
Jeremiah 31:9	
Malachi 2:10	

Summarize what you learned about God, the Father of the Old Testament.

3. Read the passages below. List the key words, or phrases, that tell us more about Yahweh as the Heavenly Father.

    Matthew 5:14-16

    Matthew 5:44-45

    Matthew 5:47-48

    Matthew 6:1-4

Memory Verse

"Because you are sons, God has sent forth the Spirit of His Son into our hearts, crying 'Abba! Father!'"

Galatians 4:6

Key Term

Pater: There are only two words for "father" in the New Testament (*with the exception of a third, used once in Heb. 7:3*). The most commonly used is the Greek word, "Pater" (*pat-ayr'*). It is the same word in Latin from which we get our English word "paternal." The other term for "father" is Aramaic and is the word "Abba" (*ab-bah'*). This word is recorded only three times in the New Testament, one of which is spoken by Jesus.

4. What are the differences we see about God between the Old and New Testaments?

Has God changed? What made the difference?

Read John 8:38

5. Jesus began referring to Yahweh as the people's Heavenly Father and as His own Father very early in His public ministry. For those who heard Jesus referring to God as their Heavenly Father, how might their perceptions of God have been challenged?

> Jesus began referring to Yahweh as the people's Heavenly Father and as His own Father very early in His public ministry.

6. How does knowing that God wants to be your personal Father affect your view of Him today?

Day 2
We Are His Daughters

THE FATHER CHOSE US

Read Galatians 3:23-4:7

7. According to Galatians 3:26, what qualifies us to be sons (children) of God?

8. As a child, through faith in Christ, what else do we become?

9. Just as a human father decided on a time for his son to be recognized as an adult, with all the rights and responsibilities of an heir (verse 2), so our Father decided on a time for us to be recognized as heirs. What happened on that date?

What is the significance of being an heir "through God" (verse 7)?

THE FATHER ADOPTS US

10. What can you learn about your adoption by God from the following verses?

Romans 8:14-16	
Romans 8:29	
Ephesians 1:3-6	
Colossians 1:12-13	
1 Peter 1:1-5	

11. How do these truths affect your view of your Heavenly Father?

12. Take a couple of minutes to thank your Heavenly Father for His plan of adoption, and the blessings that come.

Key Term

Adoption: Paul uses this word five times in the New Testament. The term "adoption" refers to the transition into becoming a son, and the relationship of becoming a child of someone.

"But as many as received Him, to them He gave the right to become children of God, even to those who believe in His name, who were born, not of blood nor of the will of the flesh nor of the will of man, but of God."
John 1:12-13

Day 3
Intimate Communication with the Father

One of the most personal and intimate activities we can engage in is prayer. Prayer provides an opportunity to consciously engage with God. Prayer is how we can communicate with our Father.

13. Read the following prayers of Jesus, and list how Christ addresses God:

Matthew 26:42	
Luke 23:34, 46	
John 11:41	

14. What does this show you about Jesus' relationship with God the Father?

Read Matthew 6:5-13

15. In Matthew 6:5-8, what are the guidelines for a healthy, intimate prayer life?

16. What can we learn from Christ's example of how to pray (verses 9-13)?

17. Prayer is not only about asking for wants and needs, it is about cultivating a relationship with our Heavenly Father. Describe the aspects from Christ's example that point you to this relationship.

> One of the most personal and intimate activities we can engage in is prayer. Prayer provides an opportunity to consciously engage with God. Prayer is how we can communicate with our Father.

18. Having looked at a proper perspective of prayer, how is your prayer life? Are there areas that you hold back or avoid taking to God in prayer? In the light of what you've studied today, consider any changes you may need to make.

Day 4
Characteristics of the Father

HE LOVES

Read Luke 15:11-32

19. Using verse 20 as a guide, what do you think the father was doing while the son was away?

20. How did the father receive his son when he returned?

21. What does this passage illustrate?

22. How does this biblical picture of God the Father compare to your personal picture?

HE PROVIDES

23. What causes you the most worry?

Notes

Read Matthew 6:25-34

24. Record ways in which our Father provides.

    What encouragement does this passage give you?

25. Describe a recent experience when you saw God as your provider.

26. Read John 6:32-40 and share how our Father provides and sustains spiritual life for His children. How does this encourage you?

HE DISCIPLINES

Read Hebrews 12:6-11

27. When your Heavenly Father disciplines, what is it likely to involve?

    Discipline has as much to do with training, tutoring, education, and instruction as it does with chastening.

    What should it produce in a child of God?

28. Compare this to the world's view of discipline. How does God's view show a true picture of love?

Deeper Knowledge

For further study into God as our Heavenly Father, look up the following verses. Describe which "fatherly" quality or act you see being displayed.

Romans 3:23-26

Romans 9:15-16

2 Corinthians 1:3-4

Titus 3:3-7

1 Peter 1:5

1 Peter 4:19

1 John 3:1

How can you be seen as thankful for Pater's work in your life? What ways can you show your thankfulness this week?

29. **Today we have seen the ways God loves, provides and disciplines. How have you experienced each one of these in your life? Take time to thank Him.**

"It is not possible to know God as Father apart from Jesus Christ."[1]

Day 5

The Fatherhood of God Shown in Christ

"That God in Christ is the only revelation of the Fatherhood of God. The revelation of God as the Father on individuals is not seen until Christ exposed it in His teachings. But more than this, Christ did not expose the Fatherhood of God by what He taught merely; He exposed the Fatherhood of God by what He was. If you reject Jesus Christ as the divine Son, and subtract Him from your conception of God you have nothing left. It is impossible to know God as the Father apart from Jesus Christ."[2]

Read John 5:16-24

30. What was Jesus' first response to the accusation in verses 16-17?

   What is the significance? (Check out Mark 2:27-28 for more input.)

31. What other statements does Jesus make that establish Himself as equal with the Father?

32. Read the following passages, and indicate the relationship of the Father and Jesus.

   Matthew 11:27

   John 10:29-30

   John 14:6

Notes

Experiencing Knowledge

33. As you have gained a better understanding of Pater, how can you minister to a sister in Christ who struggles like the woman in the opening illustration?

34. As you consider all that you've learned this week, write down at least one point that impacted you.

35. How does knowledge of this name of God lead you to trust in Him (Psalm 9:10)? What specifically will you do today to demonstrate this trust in Pater?

Reflection

Knowing God Through His Names — Lesson Twenty-One

TO KNOW HIS NAME
Conclusion – Part 1

"Pssst.... Can you keep a secret?" Few questions garner a more attentive audience. Everyone loves to hear a secret, but few manage to keep one. Personal observation confirms the Chinese saying: "What is told in the ear of a man is often heard 100 miles away."

In January 1848, an enterprising Swiss man, with plans to establish a colony in California, was eager to complete his latest construction project in Colomo. Laborers building the sawmill found more than just ordinary stones resting on the bed of the South Fork American River; they found GOLD! Foreseeing the loss of his sizable investment in the unfinished mill, General John A. Sutter implored his hired hands to keep the discovery a secret—just until the project was completed. They willingly consented...but some secrets are just too good to keep! The ensuing California Gold Rush destroyed Sutter's Mill and left the Swiss pioneer in financial ruin. In this historical event, Ben Franklin's humorous insight resonates truth: "Three may keep a secret if two of them are dead."

As you've journeyed through these last twenty lessons, you have undoubtedly made some discoveries of your own, mining numerous spiritual "nuggets" from Scripture about the character of God. Ken Hemphill captures the thrust of this year's study: "The names of God reflect God's desire to reveal Himself fully to mankind so that we might come to know Him and experience His fullness. The same is true today. God wants to reveal Himself fully to you that you might know and trust Him in every arena of your life."[1]

Learning God's name has indeed led you to a fuller understanding of Him, a greater trust in Him, and even a deeper, more meaningful worship of Him. Your view of Him has become so much bigger than when you first began this journey. As He has revealed Himself to you personally, you have grown in your intimacy with Him. Your relationship with Christ has become increasingly precious; you hold it close to your heart as a prized possession, treasuring it, desiring to protect it, delighting in this special knowledge of God.

However, unlike the laborers at Sutter's Mill, you haven't accidentally stumbled upon your great discovery. God has **ordained** your participation in this study; He has intentionally **revealed** His names to you. Like General Sutter who sought to establish a colony, God is actively building His Kingdom. So, while you may be tempted to keep this discovery all to yourself, enjoying your "secret" relationship with Him, God has bigger plans. He has revealed Himself to you for a purpose. This is one secret just too good to keep!

Day 1

These last two lessons, reflective in nature, are designed to help you review and apply what God has revealed about Himself to you through studying His names. As you complete the following questions, ask God: "What do You want me to DO with what You've revealed about Yourself?"

Elohim

We began our study with Elohim, the mighty and strong one. This plural form of El (translated God) is the Creator in Genesis who made us to know Him and have a relationship with Him. Review Elohim in Genesis 1:1-25.

1. **What is the most meaningful insight you take away from your study of God as *Elohim*, and how has it impacted you?**

Yahweh

Called by God to lead in Israel's deliverance from Egypt, a reluctant Moses meets the great "I AM." The LORD assures His chosen servant that where Moses can't, Jehovah, the self-existent One, CAN; for He is an unchanging, faithful, and truly personal God. Reread Exodus 3:1-10.

2. **What is the most meaningful insight you take away from your study of God as *Yahweh*, and how has it impacted you?**

Memory Verse

"And those who know Your name will put their trust in You, for You, O LORD, have not forsaken those who seek You."

Psalm 9:10

Day 2

El

The name El, also translated "God," is used in conjunction with other names, such as El Elyon and El Roi, adding an emphasis of God's power and might to each. Revisit Jehoshaphat in 2 Chronicles 20 as a reminder of El's amazing power and might.

   3. **What is the most meaningful insight you take away from your study of God as *El*, an how has it impacted you?**

El Elyon

In Genesis 14:20 we saw God revealed as El Elyon, God Most High. God is the exalted one, far above any other god or man. Having all the resources of heaven and earth, He can meet our every need. Review the memory verse Psalm 57:2.

   4. **What is the most meaningful insight you take away from your study of God as *El Elyon*, and how has it impacted you?**

Notes

Day 3

Adonai

Translated Lord, Adonai is our Master. Unlike the cruel slave owner who demands submission to his rule, Adonai's love motivates our willing and total surrender. Reread Genesis 15:1-6 where Abraham calls God "Adonai."

5. **What is the most meaningful insight you take away from your study of God as *Adonai*, and how has it impacted you?**

El Roi

Our God sees! He knows our circumstances and sees the condition of our hearts. Review the story of Hagar's encounter with El Roi in Genesis 16:13-16.

6. **What is the most meaningful insight you take away from your study of God as *El Roi*, and how has it impacted you?**

Notes

Day 4

El Shaddai

In Genesis 17:1-2, we see Abraham STILL waiting for his promised son. God reveals Himself to Abraham as El Shaddai. Almighty, Sovereign God is mighty to save, protect, prosper, sustain, and bless. Reread the Genesis 17:1-2 account of God's declaration to Abraham.

7. **What is the most meaningful insight you take away from your study of God as *El Shaddai*, and how has it impactd you?**

El Olam

After God reveals Himself to Abraham as El Olam in Genesis 21, Abraham places his confidence in the Eternal God instead of his treaty with Abimelech. Read Isaiah 40:28-31 to again reflect on the Everlasting God.

8. **What is the most meaningful insight you take away from your study of God as *El Olam*, and how has it impacted you?**

Notes

Jehovah Jireh

Jehovah Jireh means the Lord will provide. After asking Abraham to offer up his beloved son, God Himself provides a ram in Isaac's place. Review how God reveals Himself as Jehovah Jireh to an obedient Abraham in Genesis 22:6-14.

9. What is the most meaningful insight you take away from your study of God as *Jehovah Jireh*, and how has it impacted you?

Day 5

El Bethel

Bethel is the site where God appears to Jacob and establishes His covenant with him. God reminds Jacob of His promise when He calls Jacob back to Canaan after twenty years outside the house of God. Reread God's revelation of Himself as El Bethel in Genesis 31:1-13.

10. What is the most meaningful insight you take away from your study of God as *El Bethel*, and how has it impacted you?

Notes

Jehovah Rophe

The bitter waters of Marah provide no relief for the grumbling Israelites. God, who declares Himself the Healer, sweetens the water in response to Moses' intercessory pleas. Reexamine Jehovah Rophe in Exodus 15:22-27.

11. What is the most meaningful insight you take away from your study of God as *Jehovah Rophe*, and how has it impacted you?

Reflection

Knowing God Through His Names   Lesson Twenty-Two

Day 1

Jehovah Nissi

In the battle against the Amalekites, Moses, with staff raised, intercedes for Joshua and the Israelites. A victorious Moses names the commemorative altar Jehovah Nissi, giving full glory to God. We can also call on the Name of Jehovah Nissi to be our rallying point. Read Exodus 17:8-16.

1. **What is the most meaningful insight you take away from your study of God as *Jehovah Nissi*, and how has it impacted you?**

Jehovah M'Kadesh

Jehovah M'Kadesh is a recurring name for God in the book of Leviticus. "Kadesh" means to consecrate, sanctify, prepare, dedicate. Our holy God desires to use sanctified people to accomplish His work. Read Leviticus 20:7-8.

2. **What is the most meaningful insight you take away from your study of God as *Jehovah M'Kadesh*, and how has it impacted you?**

Day 2

Jehovah Shalom

Gideon is called by the Lord to deliver Israel from idolatry. God reassures Gideon through a sign that offers peace, revealing Himself as Jehovah Shalom. The Lord is Peace is the source for harmony in our relationship with God. Read Judges 6:1-9.

3. **What is the most meaningful insight you take away from your study of God as *Jehovah Shalom*, and how has it impacted you?**

Jehovah Sabaoth

We first see Jehovah Saboath when Hannah, desperate for a child, calls out to the Lord of Hosts. In our life's conflicts, we can likewise turn to Him for help and watch for the victory. Read 1 Samuel 1:1-11.

4. **What is the most meaningful insight you take away from your study of God as *Jehovah Saboath*, and how has it impacted you?**

Memory Verse

"And those who know Your name will put their trust in You, for You, O LORD, have not forsaken those who seek You."

Psalm 9:10

Day 3

Jehovah Raah

Psalm 23 paints a beautiful picture of Jehovah Raah. We know the Lord as Shepherd as He leads us through the trials of life. Revisit this psalm.

5. **What is the most meaningful insight you take away from your study of God as *Jehovah Raah*, and how has it impacted you?**

Jehovah Tsidkenu

Judah's repeated rebellion against God left them full of regret and utterly hopeless. Though they deserve God's unrelenting judgment, He promises to be their Jehovah Tsidkenu, the Lord Our Righteousness. Read Jeremiah 33:14-16.

6. **What is the most meaningful insight you take away from your study of God as *Jehovah Tsidkenu*, and how has it impacted you?**

Notes

Day 4

Jehovah Shammah

After the destruction of the temple and Jerusalem, Ezekiel foresees the New Jerusalem with Jehovah Shammah as the center. He will reign from His throne of truth, as we rest in His presence. Read Revelation 22:1-5.

7. What is the most meaningful insight you take away from your study of God as *Jehovah Shammah*, and how has it impacted you?

Pater

In the Old Testament, God reveals Himself as Father of the nation Israel. In the New Testament, Christ reveals God as the Father of individuals who believe in Him. Our loving Father chose us, adopted us, and wants a personal relationship with us. Review the various Scriptures in lesson 19.

8. What is the most meaningful insight you take away from your study of God as *Pater*, and how has it impacted you?

Notes

Day 5
Experiencing Knowledge

9. What names of God impacted you most and why?

10. How has studying God's names reshaped your view of who He is?

11. How has this study enhanced your understanding of Jesus?

12. How has your trust in God grown as a result of knowing His names (Psalm 9:10)?

13. What affect has knowledge of God's names had on your worship of Him?

14. What observable change(s) have you made in your life as a result of this study?

Notes

The emphasis of the "To Know His Name" study has been to know and more fully experience God, so that you will grow in trust of Him. God reveals Himself because He wants to be known.

Without question, this year's study has afforded a deeper intimate exploration of your relationship with God. While the journey has been remarkably personal, we must remember that nothing is ever about us. Everything is always about God, and what He wants to accomplish through us for the eternal good of others. In light of this principle...

What is God calling you to DO with what He's revealed about Himself this year?

Reflection

Notes

To Know His Name

Lesson 1
1. Strauss, Lehman. The Godhead. Neptune: Loizeaux Brothers, 1990.

Lesson 2
1. Hebrew Greek Key Study Bible. Chattanooga: AMG Publishers, 1996.
2. Adapted from: Strong's Concordance, Mclean: Mac Donald Publishing Company and Gensenius' Hebrew - Chaldee Lexicon to the Old Testament, Grand Rapids: Baker Book House, 1979.

Lesson 3
1. Adapted from: Hemphill, Ken. The Names of God. Nashville: Broadman and Holman Publishers, 2001. and Sumrall, Lester. The Names of God. Springdale: Whitaker House 1993.
2. Hemphill, Ken. The Names of God. Nashville: Broadman and Holman Publishers, 2001.

Lesson 4
1. Elwell, Walter A.; Comport, Philip Wesley: Tyndale Bible Dictionary. Wheaton, Ill. Tyndale House Publishers, 2001.

Lesson 5
1. Adapted from: International Standard Bible Encyclopedia. Grand Rapids: William B. Eerdman's Publishing Co, 1995.

Lesson 6
1. Stone, Nathan. Names of God. Chicago: Moody Publishers, 1944.

Lesson 9
1. Sumrall, Lester. The Names of God. Springdale: Whitaker House 1993.
2. Ibid.
3. Wiersbe, Warren. The Weirsbe Bible Commentary: New Testament, Colorado Springs: David C. Cook, 2007.

Lesson 11
1. Adapted from: Anders, Max. Holman Old Testament Commentary: Proverbs, Nashville: Broadman and Holman Publishers, 2005.

Lesson 12
1. Strauss, Lehman. The Godhead. Neptune: Loizeaux Brothers, 1990.

Lesson 13
1. Stone, Nathan. Names of God. Chicago: Moody Publishers, 1944.

Lesson 14
1. The Nelson Study Bible. Nashville: Thomas Nelson, 1997. Note on Isaiah 6:3.

Lesson 15
1. Wiersbe, Warren. The Weirsbe Bible Commentary: New Testament, Colorado Springs: David C. Cook, 2007.
2. Hemphill, Ken. The Names of God. Nashville: Broadman and Holman Publishers, 2001.
3. Lockyer, Herbert. All the Divine Names and Titles in the Bible, Grand Rapids: Zondervan Publishing House, 1988.
4. Ibid.
5. Ibid.

Lesson 16
1. Today in the Word, MBI, Oct. 1991.
2. Strauss, Lehman. The Godhead. Neptune: Loizeaux Brothers, 1990.
3. A Mighty Fortress Is Our God, by Martin Luther
4. Ibid.

Lesson 17
1. Sumrall, Lester. The Names of God. Springdale: Whitaker House, 1993.
2. Hemphill, Ken. The Names of God. Nashville: Broadman and Holman Publishers, 2001.

Lesson 18
1. Vine, W.E. Vines Expository Dictionary of Biblical Words. Nashville: Thomas Nelson, 1996.

Lesson 20
1. Stone, Nathan. Names of God. Chicago: Moody Publishers, 1944. p. 130.
2. Ibid, 130

Made in United States
Troutdale, OR
12/06/2023

15447617R00128